YOUR MONEY AND
—YOUR LIFE—

Learning how to handle money
God's way

KEITH TONDEUR

TRIANGLE

First published 1996
Triangle
SPCK
Holy Trinity Church
Marylebone Road
London NW1 4DU

Biblical translations used (in order of frequency) are:
New International Version (abbreviated as NIV)
The New American Standard Bible (NASB), published by Thomas
Nelson, Publishers, copyright the Lockman Foundation,
La Habra, California, 1977 (and earlier – maybe later too).
All rights reserved.
The Living Bible (LB), copyright 1971 Tyndale House Publishers,
Wheaton, Illinois

The publisher takes this opportunity to thank those individuals
and organizations who have given us permission to use and adapt
material for this book. Every effort has been made to trace the
owners of copyright material, though in a few cases this has proved
impossible and we apologize to any copyright holders whose rights
may have been unwittingly infringed. We trust that in the event of
any accidental infringement, the
owners of the material will contact us directly.

British Library Cataloguing in Publication Data
A catalogue record for this book is available
from the British Library

ISBN 0-281-04943-2

Typeset by Pioneer Associates, Perthshire
Printed in Great Britain by
BPC Paperbacks Ltd.

CONTENTS

To
R. T. Kendall
for showing me the unconditional
love of Jesus

ACKNOWLEDGEMENTS

There are many people I need to thank for the completion of this book. First and foremost, my wife Carole, who puts up with so much when I am in writing mode – she even managed to present me with a beautiful daughter, to join our two sons, as the book was being finished. My thanks also to Liz Lown, who somehow continues to put up with me and types and retypes all I ask with ongoing cheerfulness; to Tina Lambert, who helped with background material, and to Zoë Harmston, who gave up virtually all her summer holiday to put my years of notes into a semblance of order. I would also like to thank Tim Green, Ian Roberts and Kay Fenton for various proof readings and helpful suggestions.

Over the years a number of people have influenced me greatly, either through their writing or from personal friendship. I am therefore indebted to Larry Burkett, Howard Dayton, Gene Getz, Ronald Sider and John White from across the Atlantic and R. T. Kendall, Roy McCloughry and Rob Parsons closer to home. A number of the ideas propounded in this book originally came from them!

PREFACE

There are two opposing economic systems operating in the world today. They are humankind's economy and God's economy. Jesus taught us to love people and use things – our society appears to teach the reverse. The Bible tells us that we should not be surprised at this difference between God's way and humankind's way. Isaiah 55.8 says, "'For my thoughts are not your thoughts; neither are your ways my ways," declares the Lord' (NIV). The difference is God. In God's economy the living Lord is central. Every believer is called to be in the world but not of it. Sadly, many of us living in the West have been caught up in the materialistic society to such an extent that we are no longer focused on what the Bible says about material possessions and our lifestyle is not much different from that of those around us.

Faith in material things will not bring eternal life.

Money can be a very 'touchy' subject for many Christians. We can feel guilty if we have it and guilty if we don't. We tend to be shy about telling others how much we earn and particularly reticent about our giving. We often feel that is right that our Christian leaders tell us about holiness, sexual purity and righteous living, but we get very 'hot under the collar' when money or lifestyle issues are mentioned. Should these subjects be preached we feel indignant or uncomfortable – or both. It is almost as if our privacy has been invaded. Is this because our whole value system is being questioned?

Few Christians seem ready to acknowledge the misery caused by the misuse of money and yet the same financial worries, frustrations and anxieties that are found in the lives of non-believers are present in the lives of many Christians. When we are outside of God's will the devil can get in easily, and often in the area of finances we leave ourselves wide open to temptation. Although God has promised to provide for those who live in accordance with His plans, the pressure to compromise with materialism will lead many of us along our own route – to our detriment.

> No one is immune to financial temptation and difficulty.

The aim of this book is to help clarify God's perspective on money. I believe that for far too long we have allowed our thoughts, feelings and beliefs about financial matters to be unduly influenced by ungodly pressures. In the past what God has said about handling money has been largely ignored by Christian churches, organizations and individuals. We have become deceived into thinking that the money we earn and have in our bank account is ours. But everything belongs to God, and He will use money and possessions to direct our lives.

If money is mentioned at all in Christian circles it is usually in relation to giving. So at best some Christians may receive teaching on how to handle up to ten per cent of 'their' money. But God wants a say in how we handle the entire 100 per cent! Obviously, sharing and giving are part of God's plans for our lives but once He has our total commitment He will influence how we earn, give, save and spend the money He provides.

> The Bible is extremely practical.

In this book we are going to consider several questions and try to answer them from God's perspective. These include:

- Can a Christian be rich, or is it right that all Christians should be poor?
- Is it all right to save money, and if so for what should I save?
- How, where and when should I give?
- Should a Christian take out insurance?
- How should we handle money within our family?

Please use the 'Ask yourself' section at the end of each chapter for individual or group study. It is my hope that this book will help you to take the first steps towards following God's perfect plan for all aspects of your finances.

INTRODUCTION:
Money – Its Importance

It may surprise you to know just how much the Bible has to say about money. Although there are 500 verses on faith and a similar number on prayer there are more than 2,350 on money. Furthermore, Jesus talked about it more than anything else. Why did He have so much to say about it? After all, He lived in a much simpler society than ours – there were no credit cards or cheque books around then! I believe there are three main reasons why Jesus felt compelled to say so much about it.

1 How we handle our money affects our relationship with Jesus

In Luke 16.11 it says, 'So if you have not been trustworthy in handling worldly wealth, who will trust you with true riches?' (NIV). What Jesus is teaching here is that the way we handle our money has a direct impact on the quality of our spiritual life. If we handle our money in accordance with the principles laid down in Scripture we are going to have a much closer relationship with Jesus. Conversely, if we handle our money in a way that is contrary to His will, then our relationship is bound to suffer. This is clearly shown in the parable of the talents. The master congratulates the two servants who have managed their money faithfully. 'Well done, good and faithful servant! You have been faithful with a few things; I will put you in charge of many things. Come and share your master's happiness!' (Matthew 25.21 NIV). As we handle our money according to God's teaching we will enter into the joy of a more intimate relationship with Jesus. And it is this that is all important. If our hearts are set on God's Kingdom then any gifts we receive from Him will be secondary to being in a living, loving relationship with our Lord and with those He brings near to us – the poor, the hurt and the lost. Concern for one's neighbour arises out of a true relationship with God. It makes sense, therefore, that God's concern about wealth focuses on how it affects our relationship with Him and with our neighbour.

> It is sad that we divide the world into the sacred and the secular.

2 Money and possessions are likely to be the major competitor with Jesus for the lordship of our lives

> Western society believes that everything worth anything can be bought.

If there is any one sin that seems to dominate our society it is the relentless pursuit of material things. We have given them such a place of importance within our society that they have become our god. Once God ceases to be central and Lord of every aspect of our lives, then eternity can fade in importance, even for Christians. Jesus was accused of eating with publicans and sinners. Immoral women were put at ease in His presence. The poor sought Him out because He had come to bring them good news. Yet, sadly, so many of us choose to lock ourselves away in our middle-class churches where our buildings and religious language can so often be barriers to the very people Jesus came to save.

> Money in itself is not evil. It is only that we have made an evil use of it – we have made it our god.

But Jesus tells us that we have a choice. We cannot serve God and money. 'No-one can serve two masters. Either he will hate the one and love the other, or he will be devoted to the one and despise the other. You cannot serve both God and Money' (Matthew 6.24 NIV). Thus it is impossible to serve money in any way and still be serving the Lord.

When the Crusades were fought during the 12th century, many mercenary soldiers were paid to fight on behalf of the Crusaders. Because it was a religious war they insisted that the mercenaries were baptized before going to war, but as they were baptized they held their sword out of the water to signify that God was not in control of it. They chose to keep the freedom to do exactly as they wanted with their sword. Today many people handle their money in a similar fashion. They hold their wallets and purses 'out of the water'. In effect they are saying that God can be Lord of their lives except when it comes to their money, because they want to keep control of that themselves.

> Our faith and our finances are closely linked together.

It is important to remember that God condemns the misuse of, or the preoccupation with, money and possessions. Having money in itself is not a sin. As a matter of fact there are many examples of God blessing people abundantly. It is the *love of money* that is a root of all sorts of evil.

> If you want to know what is really important to a person look at what he or she spends his or her money on.

3 Money affects a very large part of our lives

Jesus talked so much about money because He knew just how much of our lives would revolve around it, and those of us living today are probably being affected more significantly than at any other time in history. For a few moments, just think about your normal week. How much time do you spend earning money, then making decisions about how you will spend it? How much time do you spend shopping, thinking about and reviewing your savings, and considering how much to give and where? It is precisely because we spend so much time using money and thinking about money that God has devoted so much space to it in the Bible. He wants us all to know His perfect will on the subject, and since material needs, worldly possessions and earning a living are important to all people, they provide clear openings for putting the biblical message across.

Jesus' parables alone refer to a wide variety of money issues. Just look at the sample below:

- investment (Matthew 13.44–5)
- savings (Matthew 13.52)
- debt (Matthew 18.23–35)
- earning wages (Matthew 20.1–16)
- capital and interest (Matthew 25.14–30)
- money-lending (Luke 7.41–3)
- inheritance (Luke 15.11–32)
- contrast between rich and poor (Luke 16.19–31)

God has something to say about every aspect of the way we should handle our finances, but we shy away from His teaching. Many modern Christians find it almost impossible not to prefer the apparent security of the material world to the possible risks of a life lived by faith in an invisible God. Sadly, our lifestyle often more reflects our culture than our Christianity.

Ask yourself

Look at this quote from Richard Forster's book *Money, Sex and Power*:

> When the Bible refers to money as power it does not mean something vague or impersonal. Nor does it mean power in the sense we mean when we speak, for example, of 'purchasing power'. No, according to Jesus and all the writers of the New Testament, behind money are very real spiritual forces that energise it and give it a law of its own. Hence money is an active agent, it is a law unto its own and it is capable of inspiring devotion.
>
> 1 Is money a power?
> 2 What are its dangers; its potential?
> 3 What are the dangers of letting money control our lives?

4 What impact does this have on:
   - the individual?
   - the Church?
   - society?
5 Is money your servant or master?
6 Does it form any basis for your future security?
7 Do your possessions increase or decrease your anxieties?
8 What are your basic priorities in life?
   - providing many good things for you and your family?
   - building up your assets?
   - gaining recognition from your colleagues at work?
   - making yourself 'somebody'?
   - winning people to Jesus?
   - helping the needy?
9 Does the National Lottery help good causes or encourage gambling?
10 Can there be such a thing as a rich Christian?

1 DIVIDED RESPONSIBILITY

Careful study of the Bible's teaching on finances shows that both God and we have a part to play. God retains certain responsibilities and expectations but He has delegated other responsibilities to us. Much of the pressure and frustration we experience in handling our finances comes from the fact that we do not recognize which are God's responsibilities and which are ours. First we need to understand and acknowledge God's part and then be faithful and obedient in carrying out our part. Doing this should lead to financial contentment and peace of mind.

God's part

In the Bible there are over 250 names for God. The name that probably best describes him in the area of money is Master. If we are unable to view Him as such it will affect the way we live. For example, Job was still able to worship God after losing his children and his possessions. Similarly, Moses readily gave up the treasures of Egypt and chose to suffer with the people of God. They did so because they knew the Lord and fully accepted His role as Master. There are four main aspects to God's role as Master.

1 Ownership

God owns everything. 'To the Lord your God belong the heavens, . . . the earth and everything in it' (Deuteronomy 10.14 NIV). Psalm 24.1 also tells us, 'The earth is the Lord's, and everything in it, the world, and all who live in it' (NIV). The Bible even names specific items that belong to Him, such as land (Leviticus 25.23), silver and gold (Haggai 2.8) and all the animals (Psalm 50.10–12). God is the creator of all things and He has never transferred ownership to His creation. Recognizing God's ownership of everything is a key element in allowing Jesus to become the Lord of our money and possessions. If we are going to be genuine followers of Jesus we must recognize His ownership of everything. 'In the same way, any of you who does not give up everything he has cannot be my disciple' (Luke 14.33 NIV). There are no exceptions: we must relinquish our hold on everything, including what is dearest to us. The clearest example of this is when God asked Abraham: 'Take your son, your only son, Isaac, whom you love, . . . and sacrifice him' (Genesis 22.2 NIV). When Abraham obeyed, God responded, 'Do not lay a hand on the boy . . . Now I know that you fear God, because you have not withheld from me your son, your only son' (Genesis 22.12 NIV).

When we live acknowledging God's ownership, every spending decision becomes a spiritual decision. No longer do I wonder how I will spend my money, but I ask, 'Lord, what do you want me to do with your money?' Recognizing that God owns everything should encourage us to take more care of 'our' possessions and to honour God by being environmentally and ethically responsible. Consistently acknowledging God's ownership is not easy. It is quite easy to accept it intellectually but live as if it were not true. Everything in our society, right down to the law, tells us that we possess what we own. We need a total change of mindset to start applying God's truth. Here are a few suggestions to help us recognize God's ownership.

- Pray daily for a willingness to recognize God's ownership of everything.
- Meditate daily on 1 Chronicles 29.11–12. 'Yours, O Lord, is the greatness and the power and the glory and the majesty and the splendour, for everything in heaven and earth is yours. Yours, O Lord, is the kingdom; you are exalted as head over all. Wealth and honour come from you; you are the ruler of all things' (NIV).
- Try substituting 'God's' or 'His' for 'my' and 'mine' when referring to possessions.
- Every time you buy something recognize that God owns it.

2 *Control*

The second responsibility God has retained is final control of every event that takes place on earth.

> His dominion is an eternal dominion; his kingdom endures from generation to generation. All the peoples of the earth are regarded as nothing. He does as he pleases with the powers of heaven and the peoples of the earth. No-one can hold back his hand or say to Him: 'What have you done?' (Daniel 4.34–5 NIV)

The Lord is still in control when difficulties come. 'I am the Lord, and there is no other. I form the light and create darkness, I bring prosperity and create disaster; I, the Lord, do all these things' (Isaiah 45.6–7 NIV). It is important to realize that our Heavenly Father can use apparently devastating circumstances for the ultimate good of those who love Him. 'And we know that in all things God works for the good of those who love him, who have been called according to his purpose' (Romans 8.28 NIV). This is done for several reasons:

- to prove His love
- to develop our character and trust
- to discipline us
- to demonstrate His power over the world
- to accomplish His intentions
- to provide direction for our lives

God is in control of every circumstance we will ever face. We can rest assured knowing that our loving Heavenly Father is in control of every situation, each of which He intends to use for a good purpose. Therefore He will *never*:

- use money to worry us. If we are worried about money we are not allowing God to have full control.
- allow money to corrupt us. A Christian, therefore, whose financial life is characterized by greed, pride or deceit is out of God's will.
- let money boost our ego.

- allow us to hoard money. Those who are looking for security in this way are looking in the wrong place.
- permit us to satisfy every whim. There is nothing spiritual about poverty, but God does not want us to live in over-indulgence whilst His work needs money and other Christians go without food and clothing. We can live well but our commitment to Christ should make us live differently.

> 'Money is like muck, no good except it be spread.'
> (Francis Bacon, 1561–1620, English philosopher)

3 Provision

The third element of God's part is provision. God has promised to supply all our *needs*. 'But seek first his kingdom and his righteousness, and all these things will be given to you as well' (Matthew 6.33 NIV). The same God who gave manna to the Children of Israel in the wilderness and fed 5,000 with only five loaves and two fish has promised to supply our needs. In this God is both predictable and unpredictable. He is totally predictable in His faithfulness in providing for our needs, but we can never be certain just how He will do it. He can use various methods such as increasing our income, changing our lifestyle or through gifts from others. Whatever way He chooses will be both perfect and reliable for our situation.

It is important here to quantify the difference between needs and wants. In our materialistic society we are bombarded daily with dozens of advertisements telling us how many different things we 'need'. In fact, we hardly 'need' any of them at all. A need is a basic necessity of life – food, clothing and a roof over our heads. A want is anything over and above that. 'But if we have food and clothing, we will be content with that' (1 Timothy 6.8 NIV). God may well give us many of our wants as well but He has not promised to provide them.

God works through provision. We may be asked to help satisfy the needs of others. If we have never learned to give sacrificially God cannot give back. He may also want us to draw closer to other Christians, and therefore He will use our abundance to supply the needs of others, and at another stage in life He may even reverse the relationship.

4 *Allocation*

The last element of God's part is that He allocates possessions to whomever and in whatever quantity He chooses. He loves us all equally but does not give possessions equally to all his children. This is clearly demonstrated in the parable of the talents. 'To one He gave five talents of money, to another two talents, and to another one talent, each according to his ability' (Matthew 25.15 NIV). And not only does God give us possessions, He also sometimes permits them to be taken from us. 'The Lord gave and the Lord has taken away; may the name of the Lord be praised' (Job 1.21 NIV).

Fundamental to a Christian perspective is that notwithstanding the different amounts given they are all gifts from God to be used in His service.

Matthew 11.28 says, 'Come to me, all you who are weary and burdened, and I will give you rest. Take my yoke upon you . . . For my yoke is easy and my burden is light' (NIV). God does not expect any of us to carry burdens only He is capable of bearing. God has assumed all burdens of ownership, control, provision and allocation. To some degree we probably all realize this mentally, but then largely fail to live it out, and consequently suffer so many negative emotions. But we need to accept God's part fully before we look at the responsibilities He has placed upon us.

The more we know about God's will the more accountable we are to live up to the light we have.

Our part

The word that best describes our part is steward. In the Bible a steward has great responsibility. He is the supreme authority under the master and has full responsibility for all his master's possessions and household affairs. God has given human beings the authority to be stewards. 'You made him ruler over the works of your hands; you put everything under his feet' (Psalm 8.6 NIV).

What is Christian stewardship?

Christian stewardship is very much about challenging attitudes and ethics of ownership. Jesus said we can either put our relationship with God first or we can put our possessions first. We cannot do both at the same time. It is much easier when our faith comforts us and confirms our views; it is not so easy when it stimulates and challenges us. Christian stewardship is a life commitment to real care for one another, to living generously and to practical care for our environment. It is:

- praising God for the whole of His creation
- regarding our whole lives, our work and our possessions as gifts from God to be used in His service
- viewing the earth's resources as riches to be used responsibly for all humankind
- being responsible for sharing in Christ's mission to the world and thus helping others come to Christ

> As stewards we are accountable to God.

It is out of this understanding of stewardship that we recognize that everything is from God, and thus we want not only to thank Him but to handle the resources given to us in the best possible way – His way. He may ask us to make material sacrifices and to endure hardship in the process, but He also promises great blessings. He is not ordering us to live a life of poverty, He is challenging us to live a life of obedience and gratitude.

Jesus urges us to have an attitude of holding possessions lightly, being faithful to Him and also open-hearted and open-handed to people in need. His faith had to be practical and not bogged down in religious minutiae. Ours should be the same. He taught the importance of good stewardship for all. Each of us is answerable to Him for how we live, our priorities, our values, the choices we make, and for how we handle our money and possessions. Words that do much to help our understanding of stewardship are found in Micah 6.8: 'And what does the Lord require of you? To act justly and to love mercy and to walk humbly with your God' (NIV). Stewardship is not just to be practised in the church but also in the office, the supermarket and in the home.

Lazarus is still with us, sleeping rough in our cities. He may not ask us directly for help, no one may ask on his behalf. Sometimes he may be round the corner out of sight or his picture may come into our living-room via the television screen. How does this affect us? Jesus clearly taught that whatever excess possessions God allows Christians to accumulate should be used creatively to further His Kingdom. This leads to some highly relevant questions:

- What is excessive in terms of the house we live in, the car we drive or the clothes we wear?
- How much do we need to plan for the future?
- How much insurance should we have?
- How much provision do we need to make for our children?

In many societies these questions are answered automatically. People live and die with barely sufficient to meet their basic needs. But for those of us who live in affluent parts of the world there are no ready answers. Each Christian has to address these questions individually in prayer and meditation on God's word.

> If God tells you to give it all away do so. If He tells you to share with others do so. If He tells you to keep it all for yourself then you have not heard from God.

The relationship between our stewardship and our place in heaven

There is a relationship between our effectiveness as stewards on earth and our place in heaven. In our everyday living we must deal with everything that is entrusted to us, be it money, time or giving, in the light of an eternal viewpoint. Remember, there can be injustice when we fail to do for others what they cannot do for themselves.

> When money speaks the truth is often silent.

Whenever we put money first in our lives, when wealth and possessions become our master, then we are likely to do things which hurt other people. We have to consider what is more important – money and possessions or others who are made in the likeness of Christ. We cannot serve two masters, because they oppose each other. Of course, this does not mean that we should all leave work and get rid of all our possessions, but rather that we should be on our guard in case any of these things becomes our god. Money and possessions have a subservient place and we should ensure that they remain there.

Whenever there is a gulf between what we say with our lips and how we behave, between what we do in church and what we do elsewhere, we have the contrast between belief and application that Jesus so strongly criticized. The condemnation of the Laodicean church – that it was materially content, but spiritually blind – could well apply to many of us. We may worship God faithfully in church without it impacting on us and enabling us to grow. If the way we live has no impact on our community then we could be better stewards.

> The possession of wealth places heavy responsibility on us.

Our responsibility is to be faithful

Before we can be faithful we need to examine the Bible to see how God wants us to handle His possessions. First of all, God wants us to be faithful, regardless of how much He has entrusted to us. In the parable of the talents (Matthew 25.14–30), the master gave his stewards different sums of money but when he returned he held each of them accountable for how he had managed his possessions. Interestingly, the steward who had been given the two talents received the same reward as the steward who had been given five talents (Matthew 25.21–3). Therefore, it is clear that God rewards faithfulness regardless of the amount we have been entrusted with. We are required to be faithful with much or little.

> It's not what I'd do if a million pounds were my lot. It's what I am doing with the five pounds that I've got!

God wants us to be faithful in handling *all* the money entrusted to us. For years most of the little teaching we have received on money has been in the area of giving, and although this is vitally important, we have, by default, allowed Christians to learn to handle the rest of their money from a worldly perspective. This has serious consequences because our response to God, our commitment to Christ, our concern for our neighbour and our own spiritual state are all closely linked with the way we think about and manage our money and possessions.

We are known and loved but we are also accountable. Psalm 139.1–3 tells us, 'O Lord, you have searched me and you know me. You know when I sit and when I rise; you perceive my thoughts from afar. You discern my going out and my lying down; you are familiar with all my ways' (NIV). There is nothing past, present or future that God doesn't know about us. The One who knows you the best also loves you the most. But 2 Corinthians 5.9–10 reads, 'So we make it our goal to please him . . . For we must all appear before the judgment seat of Christ, that each one may receive what is due to him for the things done while in the body, whether good or bad' (NIV). This should motivate us to handle our money more in accordance with God's will. Our life on earth is but a blink of an eye when compared to eternity, yet how we live on earth has an impact throughout eternity.

> It is the shrewd who handle their money wisely. They save well, do not borrow at high interest rates, buy sensibly and never over-commit themselves.

As Christians we are called to be generous to those from whom we cannot expect anything, even including love and thanks, in return (Luke 6). I believe our joy in heaven will be proportionate to our place there and our place there will be largely dependent upon how we have lived on earth and who we have won for Christ. When we die it is they who will welcome us into the Kingdom and we will have for ever to rejoice. Already, as I look back on my life, nothing seems as important as the people I have introduced to Jesus. Constantly we need to ask ourselves, 'What will this do for eternity?'

> A changed life is the true evidence of salvation.

Materialism

It is not possessing riches that God condemns but clinging to them, coveting them and centring our lives around them. For example, there is nothing wrong in making our church buildings pleasant places in which to meet, but if all our efforts, time and money are being used to maintain them then something is wrong. Most of us are too possession-centred. We think it is our right to acquire them. We readily go into debt to accumulate them and work longer and longer hours for the 'benefits' that they bring. They enslave our bodies, hearts and minds, and can so easily leave us spiritually dry and with no room for the needy, the starving and the dying.

> Many when asked, 'How much is enough?' reply 'Just a little more'.

So we often strive for things even as we talk of heaven. And we feel guilty as we wonder whether we should be sharing more with our brothers and sisters in need. Perhaps we blame others for economic mismanagement, but then we think of the early Christians lovingly and generously selling to help meet the needs of others and our guilt compounds as we start to apologize for our new cars and large houses. For years when I read the passages in the Bible about rich people I would feel sorry for the Royal Family! Then one day it dawned on me that I thought of a rich person as someone who had much more than I had. I believe most people do the same. We may argue that we do not want outrageous wealth, just a reasonable degree of financial security, but we don't want to miss out on anything either. We may say we only want enough without realizing that we keep redefining 'enough' as our income grows. In world-wide terms most of us in the West are rich. These Bible passages apply to you and me!

> We worship money, material things, sex and power. We refer to money as 'the bottom line' and gauge our success in society by the kind of houses, cars and furniture we possess.

The rich young ruler had to sell all he had and follow Jesus to gain eternal life but he just couldn't do it (Matthew 19.16–22). He loved his possessions which he could see, and he lacked faith in an invisible God. He was not condemned for possessing riches, only for hanging on to them as if they were a life-raft in a stormy sea.

Materialism makes it impossible to listen to and apply the whole gospel. It prevents us from putting Christ first, and if we do not put Him first He can be nowhere else. Furthermore, a Church which has compromised with materialism cannot confront the powers which are generating it within our society. The evils of poverty and escape into private security remain unchallenged if the Church, which is called to be a prophetic and distinctive voice in the world, is not distinguishable from it. The more we absorb the world's values the less able we are to challenge them.

The claim that material possessions provide security is a myth. The rich have as many problems arising out of their humanity as do the poor. But materialism:

- offers the rich person another kingdom with self as king
- creates anxiety
- tries to conform us to others
- leads to guilt which can seriously damage our faith

Materialism can never deliver what it promises. Jesus said, 'Do not be anxious about tomorrow' so why are so many anxious? He says, 'Your Heavenly Father knows you need these things', so why do so many of us feel insecure?

> The temptation to believe that happiness, peace of mind, maturity, forgiveness and love can be bought is a seductive fantasy.

In our society, as never before, we are bombarded by consumerism. It affects us via television, radio, press and the high street. Look at some of the aspects of it:

The wallet (prosperity)
Happiness comes through acquiring certain good things in life. Your dream is one day to win the National Lottery.

The new car (success)
This cries out, 'I'm someone who's made it in life.' 'I'm successful.' 'People look up to me.'

The supermarket shelf (freedom of choice)
I have the right to choose whatever I want, be it tins of food, school, house, car, sexual partner or whatever. It is my right to choose and I can have what I want, when I want it. Don't interfere in my life or mention responsibilities.

The credit card (instant gratification)
Why should I have to wait? I want the same things as my colleagues and neighbours and I want them now. Why should I bother to save? If I want to change my house/my car/whatever I'll do it *now*.

We are being sold a justification of material self-gratification which is remarkable only for its total shallowness.

Sadly, we seem to be obsessed with the individualism of the culture we live in. We spend our money and then spend even more hoping that we will be able to earn it tomorrow. We reach out for an ever increasing array of different produce which is eagerly pushed towards us. Abundance in our society has become such a threat that people will steal, or even, in extreme cases, kill for what they want. As more and more is produced so we have to be persuaded that we 'need' more and more. Of course goods should be available and distributed effectively, but we are talking of an overabundance. Every day in parts of the world children starve to death. As Christians we have to ask ourselves how necessary it is for us to follow fashion in cars and clothes. How much does hair-style or hemline matter? Beware – advertising so often plays on our anxieties, greed, guilt and snobbery.

As Christians our values often reflect the values of the society we live in.

While some people are spoilt for choice, others have no choice. The rich have considerable power over their own lives, while the poor have simply to accept what life offers them. However, poor people can be very materialistic and long for things beyond their grasp. One only has to look at the sales of National Lottery tickets to confirm this. For those of us who are better off the way we live is a personal expression of who we are, and that is why we feel so easily threatened if someone criticizes the way we live. It is important that we ask the right questions. For example, the question is not 'How can I identify with the poorest people on earth?' but 'How should I live, given their existence?'

> 'I know how very hard it is to be rich and still keep the milk of human kindness. Money has a dangerous way of putting scales on one's eyes, a dangerous way of freezing people's hands, eyes, lips and hearts.' (Dom Helder Camara, born 1909, Brazilian theologian and bishop)

The centre of consumerism is always self. It is the 'I want' syndrome. I want more pleasure, more comfort, more things. *Self, self, self.* This is probably the worst four-letter word in existence. It is the primary cause of failure towards God, partner, children and others. Every time we seek self-gratification we take some of the deserved glory away from our Lord. A person with £10 can be more selfish than someone with £10 million – it all depends on attitude. How do you feel if a guest breaks something of value? Do you feel more upset about your loss than you do about your friend's embarrassment?

Consumerism can be a hunger within us. The more we feed it the more it grows and the more hungry we become. And the more we live as part of the world the easier it will be for consumerism totally to dethrone God as Master of our lives. Wealth and possessions can make it difficult for a person to acknowledge their need of God but, as the story of Zacchaeus shows, they can still be reached.

> Material things do not provide ultimate happiness nor do they last for ever.

Lifestyle issues

> 'The world asks "What does a man own?" Christ asks "How does he use it?"' (Andrew Murray, 1828–1917, South African evangelistic preacher)

Even if we give regularly we are contradicting our gifts if we choose to live dishonestly and unethically. Neither will generous giving cancel out the results of a lifestyle that conforms to this world's system of values. God wants us to do His will in all respects.

John Wesley's teaching

There was one word that John Wesley hated – 'afford'. People would say, 'But I can afford it' when he preached against extravagance in food, dress or lifestyle. He argued that no Christian should be able to afford things other than the bare necessities of life, because all else should be given to God. His argument goes as follows:

1   God is the source of all the Christian's money. He is the one who has given us our energy and intelligence. He is the true source of all our wealth.

2   As Christians we must account to the Lord for how we have used our money. At any time we may be called and will have to give an account to the Lord for the way in which we have used the wealth God has given us. Because none of us know when this will be we cannot waste money now, planning to make it up to God later.

3   As Christians we are stewards of God's money. The money in our hands is not ours but His. We do not own it, rather we are His agents in distributing it. Thus we must use it not as we wish but as He directs.

4   God gives Christians money for them to pass it on to those who need it. God's purpose in giving us money is for us to help the poor and needy. To use it on ourselves is therefore to steal from both God and them.

5   Christians may no more buy luxuries for themselves than they may throw their money away. God made us trustee of His resources so we may feed the hungry and clothe the naked in His name. We should turn our extra money into food and clothing for the poor. Just as it would be wrong

to destroy other people's food and clothes so it would be wrong to spend money needlessly on ourselves.

Right and wrong financial thinking

The following are signs of correct financial thinking:

- using material possessions in harmony with the will of God. This will have a profound unifying effect on the Body of Christ.
- Christians with significant possessions showing humility
- sharing possessions to help meet human need
- using our homes for hospitality
- trusting God but at the same time doing our part to be responsible Christians

One of the most obvious facts that stands out in the Bible is that our lifestyle should have an effect upon non-Christians and should demonstrate our love for God and for each other. This encourages others to seek Him as Saviour. We should use what goods we have differently. We will want our settees to be sat on and our carpets walked on and we will want to share our food and drink with others. The visitor will always be more important than the possession. The question is not whether owning X or Y is wrong, but what message is conveyed by our attitude towards our possessions.

> It is possible to become extremely rich, enjoying every comfort which modern society can provide, and yet still live an impoverished life.

The following is a long list of indications of wrong financial thinking:

- overdue bills
- worrying about savings or assets
- a 'get-rich-quick' attitude
- a lack of desire to work

- dishonesty
- greed – someone who can never put another person first suffers from greed. A Christian who cannot put aside his or her own wants to satisfy the needs of others suffers from greed.
- covetousness – desiring what belongs to someone else or 'trying to keep up with the Joneses'
- unfulfilled family needs – when basic needs like food and clothing cannot be met because of debts elsewhere.
- unfulfilled Christian needs – unfortunately this appears to be the norm in today's society but it is our responsibility to meet the needs of those who cannot do so themselves.
- over commitment to work – many Christians' lives are dominated by work. God's plan for work is excellence not excess.
- self-indulgence – purchasing without regard to the costs, living a lavish lifestyle, constantly trading in cars and domestic appliances for newer models, filling extensive wardrobes with seldom-worn clothes and spending frivolously in the sales
- lack of commitment to God's work
- an attitude of financial superiority – having a lot of money is not a right, but a responsibility.
- an attitude of financial resentment – I believe it is very dangerous to ask God to give us what we 'deserve' – he might just do so!

> When we turn our finances over to God we must be willing to accept his direction.

Wealth and poverty

> Many Christians are trying to 'make it to the top' without having any idea what they will find when they get there.

Wealth can be creative, being used to spread God's word and help the poor and needy, or it can be wasted, spent on frivolous activities, lavish living and gambling. Wealth can also be corruptive, being used to bribe, trade illegally or buy guns and bombs. There are many examples throughout the Bible of money being used for good. But just as there is potential for good there are real dangers. Money is a power – just think of big business and the National Lottery. Money also has power at an individual level and this is why we take it so personally. It seems very unnatural to talk about how much we earn or to admit to our financial difficulties.

In defining wealth we usually compare ourselves with the people around us and this is largely dictated by the area in which we live. Therefore it is easy to create a false picture of our relative wealth or poverty. However, there are certain indicators of wealth which we tend to see as symbols of who we are and how we see ourselves. Such indicators include property, possessions, cars, salary, education, career, holidays and savings.

> As the 'consumer culture' pressurizes us to acquire more, 'having' increasingly becomes more important than 'being'.

Wealth distribution

Wealth can be distributed in our society in various different ways:

- Inheritance – most people in Britain will receive some form of inheritance from their family.
- Employment – there is no doubt that work is the major source of distribution.
- Taxation – one of the prime aims of this is to take wealth from high earners and provide services and support for the underprivileged.
- Social Security – payment of state benefit through various, usually means-tested, criteria.
- Windfalls – e.g. gambling.

- Education – where qualifications can lead to higher income.
- Charity – donations to help meet specific needs.
- Interest – money earned on savings.

> 'Where money is an idol to be poor is a sin.' (William Stringfellow, American Christian author)

Wealth brings with it responsibilities and duties. The world says that wealth means 'life is secure and all I have earned is mine'. But God's way is different. All wealth is His. He enabled you to produce it. All wealth is held in trust for God and your money represents the life you choose.

> Most individual tension, family friction, anger and frustration are caused directly or indirectly by money.

Jesus' sayings about wealth and possessions are often said to be the hardest in the Gospel. He criticized the money-lenders and the well-off Pharisees. He encouraged people to have a detachment from wealth and possessions. Yet He did not idealize poverty. His compassion for those in need is well known and His pleas to those who love Him to share with the needy is a central plank of His teaching – and there has never been a greater need than there is today.

I have never been hungry for more than 24 hours except when I have voluntarily chosen to be so. I have never had to go without food, clean water and shelter. I have never had to turn down my child's request for a basic need. Few in Britain have. But I know of some who have been so deeply in debt that they could see no way of getting out of it, and yet they have felt they had to go ever deeper to try. I know of others evicted from their homes, fearful that their children will be taken into care. I know of people losing three jobs in a year, losing benefits, and all the time the bills are mounting up. There is plenty of poverty in this world:

- 100 million people have nowhere to live.
- 770 million don't eat enough to be able to work.

- 1,300 million have no safe water to drink.
- 14 million children die of starvation every year.
- The richest 20 per cent of the world's population living in the industrially advanced nations have average incomes 30 times higher than the poorest 20 per cent.

Just writing down these figures makes me feel spiritually bereft. It simply is not possible to love God while we neglect the suffering of our neighbours.

> 'Jesus tells us that people who cry because their hearts are broken over the things that break the heart of God are the fulfilled people in this world.' (Tony Campolo, American professor of sociology and author)

Poverty is not something we are called to – unless it is for a greater end. We are not called to imitate Christ's poverty but to follow Him in His example of love and self-giving, not caring whether we are poor or rich so long as we are following Him and obediently doing His will. Similarly, abundance may or may not represent God's goodness. It could indicate hard work, inheritance or even dishonest behaviour. We must never assume that to be wealthy is *ipso facto* to be in God's good books. There are extremely wicked rich people just as there are godly rich.

> 'If anyone does not refrain from the love of money he will be defiled by idolatry and so be judged as if he were one of the heathen.' (Polycarp, 70–156, Bishop of Smyrna)

The benefits of handling money faithfully

There are several benefits of handling money faithfully:

A more intimate relationship with Jesus
Remember what the master said to the steward who had been faithful in discharging his financial responsibilities: 'Enter into the

joy of your master'. As we are faithful so we will know Jesus better.

Development of character

We can either become the master of money or it can control us. God takes money, or the lack of it, and tests us with it, as He moulds us to be more like Jesus. The Bible regards the way a person handles money as a good guide to their true character. We all know the expression, 'money talks', and it does. In fact by examining a person's cheque book you can learn far more about them than by listening to them talk! After all at the end of the day we spend money on the things that are most important to us.

Learning contentment

Contentment is mentioned seven times in the Bible and on six occasions it is in relation to money. One of the main aims of this book is to help you become financially content. 'I have learned the secret of being content in any and every situation, whether well fed or hungry, whether living in plenty or in want' (Philippians 4.12 NIV). Look carefully at this verse: contentment is not something we are born with, it is something we have to learn.

Having our finances in order

As we apply biblical principles to our finances we will begin to get out of debt, spend more wisely and start saving for future goals. We will also be able to give more to the work of Christ.

Some important principles of faithfulness

If we waste possessions God can remove us as stewards

'There was a rich man whose manager was accused of wasting his possessions. So he called him in and asked him, "What is this I hear about you? Give an account of your management, because you cannot be manager any longer"' (Luke 16.1–2 NIV). First, we should note that when we waste our possessions this can easily become public knowledge ('What is this I hear about you?') and so be a poor testimony. Second, God can remove us as stewards if we squander what He has given us. There is a deep gulf between Christian stewardship and the acquisitiveness which hoards on the one hand and engages in conspicuous consumption on the other.

Faithfulness in small things is essential
'Whoever can be trusted with very little can also be trusted with much, and whoever is dishonest with very little will also be dishonest with much' (Luke 16.10 NIV). If you want to know how a person will do a big job see how he handles a small one first. Someone once said, 'Small things are small things, but faithfulness with a small thing is a big thing!'

It is important to be faithful with another's possessions
Faithfulness with another's possessions will to some degree determine how much you are given. 'And if you have not been trustworthy with someone else's property, who will give you property of your own?' (Luke 16.12 NIV). Are you faithful with the possessions of others – your family's, your friends', your boss's?

Summary

Money can be a master:

- a rival god (Matthew 6.24)
- a root of evil (1 Timothy 6.9–11)
- a deception (Revelation 3.16–17)

Or it can be a servant:

- a blessing for you (Ecclesiastes 5.19)
- a blessing for others (Luke 6.38)
- a way of obtaining true spiritual riches (Luke 16.10–12)

It is very much my hope that as you read through the next few chapters of this book you will be able to make money a servant in both your attitudes and actions.

'The fellow that has no money is poor. The fellow that has nothing but money is poorer still.' (Billy Sunday, 1862–1935, American revivalist)

Ask yourself

1 Is there a connection between Christian maturity and freedom from possessions and possessiveness?
2 Think about one particular possession – say your car.
  – Why choose that make and model?
  – How do you feel when you drive it?
  – What do you think it might be saying about you?
3 Think about the clothes you wear.
  – Why did you choose them?
  – How do you feel when you wear them?
  – How fashion-conscious are you?
  – What do you think your clothes say about you?
4 Can you give a clear statement of your own set of values?
5 Are you using your home for hospitality?
6 Paul tells us to be content in all things. How would you feel if you lost your job, your house, your money? How easily would you adapt?
7 Are you modelling the way Christians should use their material possessions?
8 How affected are you by the consumerist society we live in?

2 BUDGETING

> 'A budget tells your money where to go, otherwise you wonder where it went.' (J. Edgar Hoover, 1895–1972, Director FBI)

One of the best ways of demonstrating sound financial control is to budget your finances. Everyone should be doing this, especially Christians, as it demonstrates good stewardship. So this is for all – not just for those who are in debt or struggling to make ends meet. We *all* need to be responsible.

'Whoever can be trusted with very little can also be trusted with much, and whoever is dishonest with very little will also be dishonest with much. So if you have not been trustworthy in handling worldly wealth, who will trust you with true riches?' (Luke 16.10–11 NIV)

This short passage raises awkward questions for us all:

- Am I always totally honest in my financial dealings however small?
- Am I always totally honest with the taxman, my employer, my family?
- Am I trustworthy with the money God has given me?
- Do I ever waste money?
- To whom and how much should I give?
- Would Jesus have the same priorities as I do?

Often people are reluctant to begin to budget because they are afraid of the truth it will reveal. We don't know where our money goes because we don't look – and we don't look because we really don't want to know! Budgeting is often regarded as an enemy – something that will bring loss of freedom and many hours of unrelieved boredom. But this certainly need not be the case.

If you are not budgeting, then at best you are handling your money by 'guestimates' and at worst you are just hoping for the best. This is neither spiritually nor practically sound. Living by a budget will undoubtedly make your money go further. When you fail to budget there is frequently 'too much month left at the end of the money'. Once you have worked out a budget that will help to guide and restrain your spending, you should find it much easier to stay in control. Remember too that when you first budget it will start showing where you really spend your money. You may imagine that you are spending on priorities such as your children's clothing, but quite often it will be revealed that newspapers, chocolate and video films are more important in your life than you realized!

Obviously, a budget is only useful if it is accurate and if you keep to it. For example, if you are eating three Mars Bars a day and not recording them, then your budget is likely to be pounds out (and you are likely to be pounds heavier) by the end of the month. The main reason for recording *all* your income and expenditure is to determine accurately what you are actually earning and spending. The best way of doing this is for all members of the family who are old enough to be responsible to carry a small notebook with them at all times to record all spending. At the end of each day enter it into a monthly sheet as shown in the example in Table 1. Study it carefully before you begin to fill in your own sheet.

The importance of budgeting

At this stage many may still fail to realize the importance of budgeting. You may still think you know where your money goes – even if your biggest expenditure item is 'miscellaneous'! It is so easy to make a major miscalculation and you could be struggling for months, if not years, to put it right. Don't believe me? Then try the following exercise. It would be particularly beneficial to

Table 1 Record of monthly spending

Day	Giving	Mortgage/rent	Council tax	Insurance	Gas/electricity	Phone	TV/video	Car/travel	Saving	Loan & credit cards	Food/drink	Hobbies/entertainment	Christmas/birthdays	Holiday	Clothes	Repairs/decoration	Misc.	TOTAL
1	50																	50
2											2							2
3			20															20
4											2							2
5								20			68							88
6																		
7						90					3							93
8																		
9									30									30
10		200																200
11					100							6						106
12																		
13											3							3
14																		
15																		
16													30		70			100
17								32			2							34
18					40													40
19																95		95
20																		
21							30	75										105
22															15		10	25
23																		
24																		
25								15										15
26												40						40
27																		
28								4										4
29																		
30																		
31								18										18
	50	200	20		140	90	30	164	30		80	46	30		85	95	10	1070

do this with your partner if you are married. Husbands and wives tend to have different priorities and there often needs to be compromise as the available money is juggled to meet the many calls made upon it.

Christmas budget

Imagine you are a 'nuclear' family – mum, dad and two children. Off the top of your head write down the *total extra* amount you think the family will spend over the Christmas and New Year period. If you have thought about it for more than ten seconds you are disqualified!

Now think about and discuss with your partner what you think the family would spend in the following areas:

- food
- drinks
- presents
- wrapping paper, cards, postage
- Christmas tree and decorations
- going out (office dinners, pantomime, etc.)
- travel (visiting relatives)
- January sales

How did you do? If you thought the family would spend an extra £600 but when you added it up it came to only £500, then things are fine because you still have £100 in the bank. However, it usually works out that if you thought they would spend an extra £600 and they actually spent an extra £1,600, then the family is in debt to the tune of £1,000. They could well have overspent at the bank or, more likely, they will have used credit or store cards. If this is the case they could also be facing interest rates in excess of 20 per cent. In addition, it always seems inevitable that heavy gas and electricity bills arrive at the same time!

Budgeting is vital because without it it is so easy to fall into debt. We all need to think carefully about every item of heavy expenditure. As with all spending, there are no right and wrong answers as to how much should be spent at Christmas. It is entirely up to you, your partner, your budget and your relation-ship with God in establishing where your priorities lie. But people who are financially free manage their money by design not default.

Your estimated budget

Tables 2A and 2B include a form which will enable you to com-plete your estimated budget. To do so you should study the totals of each column of your income and expenditure lists produced earlier to get reasonably accurate estimates. As you enter your income and expenditure, try and be as accurate as you can but do not be too pedantic about ensuring precise amounts at this

Table 2A **Your personal budget: Details of monthly income**

Your basic salary	£
Spouse's basic salary	£
Guaranteed overtime	£
(Flexible overtime)*	£
(Flexible bonuses)*	£
Pension	£
Child benefit	£
Income support	£
Family credit	£
Other benefits	£
Maintenance	£
Disability benefits	£
TOTAL INCOME	£

* Put in brackets but do not add to total as these figures cannot be relied on week after week. When they occur use to pay off debts or save as appropriate.

Please note
In the following statement of monthly expenditure non-essential items have been included as they need to be calculated for budgeting purposes and to enable you to see areas where you might be able to cut back. However, if you are in debt it should be remembered that county court guidelines allow non-essential expen-diture to be struck off your financial statement. Creditors will also expect you to cut back all you can.

stage. Real accuracy will develop only as you maintain records over a period of time. Remember you probably have several items that you pay by direct debit or standing order on a monthly or annual basis – so include them in your expenditure total.

Table 2B   **Your personal budget: Details of monthly expenditure**

Formal commitments

Regular giving	£	TV licence	£
Mortgage	£	Car MOT	£
Rent	£	Road tax	£
Water rates	£	Vehicle insurance	£
Ground rent	£	Regular saving	£
Service charge	£	Personal insurance	£
Council tax	£	Private pension	£
Property insurance	£	Maintenance payments	£
Home contents insurance	£	Second mortgage	£
Electricity	£	Loan repayments	£
Gas	£	HP repayments	£
Oil	£	Credit card payments	£
Coal	£	School fees	£
Telephone	£	Other	£

Formal commitments – total 1	£

Everyday spending

Food and sundries	£	TV rental	£
Children's pocket money	£	Video rental	£
Childminder	£	Evening classes	£
Toys and books	£	Tapes and CD's	£
Pet food	£	Alcohol	£
Laundry/dry cleaning	£	Cigarettes	£
Chemist	£	Newspapers &	
Petrol	£	magazines	£
Parking	£	Other	£
Public transport	£		

Everyday spending – total 2	£

Occasional costs

Christmas	£	Vet bills	£
Birthdays	£	Clothing	£
Holidays	£	Dentist	£
Car repairs	£	Optician	£
House repairs	£	Trips & outings	£
Redecoration	£	Meals out	£
Replacement furniture	£	Other	£

Occasional costs – total 3   £

TOTAL MONTHLY EXPENDITURE

Total 1:	£
Total 2:	£
Total 3:	£

GRAND TOTAL   £

Balance

Monthly income:	£
Monthly expenditure	£
Monthly surplus / deficit	£

Hints

1 The estimated budget has been designed with many categories to help jog your memory in case you have overlooked any spending. You will almost certainly not be spending in every category.

2 It is good to get your budget as accurate as it can be as soon as possible. Therefore the more bills you can pay on a monthly basis the better.

3 For those bills that you still have to pay quarterly, put aside one-third of their estimated cost in your monthly budget. Similarly, divide any annual payments by twelve and again put that figure in your monthly budget. This represents money that you have but cannot spend because you have to set it aside until the bill falls due.

Determine whether your budget is in surplus or deficit

After ensuring your budget is complete, you need to add up your total expenditure and deduct it from your total income. If your income is more than you spend, the number will be positive and you probably have permission to feel slightly relieved! For many of us, however, the figure will be in deficit. This means that we are currently spending more each month than we earn, and this explains why the money runs out before the end of the month.

This estimated budget is important. Before you did it you probably did not fully realize what you are spending. Having completed the budget you may well have had a nasty surprise, as it could so easily reveal that there is considerable over-spending and you may well be afraid that you will never be able to make it balance. If this is your situation then please do not despair. As I have said before many, if not most, people when they first realize their situation are in a similar position. We will soon be looking at ways of rectifying the situation, but if you are at all uneasy get in touch with us at Credit Action or go to your local money advice centre straight away.

Irregular income

I have often had people say to me that they cannot budget because their income is so irregular. With the greatest respect, that is even more reason to budget. For example, if you are self-employed or a salesperson largely reliant on commission you need to make a conservative estimate as to what your annual income will be and then divide by twelve to determine your average monthly income. It is especially important for those whose income is irregular to try and set up a reserve of short-term savings from which a steady income can be drawn in 'bad' months. The biggest challenge for those with unpredictable income is to save the extra income in the 'good' months.

Adjusting the budget

As mentioned earlier, many discover on completion of their budget that their current spending – including giving, savings, debt repayments and everyday expenditure – adds up to more than their current income. To balance your budget you must increase your income or reduce your expenditure, or both. So your next job is to try and adjust your family budget so that it balances. However, before you try and do this have a look at how the Joe Bloggs family were able to adjust their budget (see Tables 3A and 3B). Here are some hints.

The first thing to do is to review each income and expenditure category. Can you think of any ways of increasing income? Then ask yourself two questions about each spending category. Is this really needed? If it is needed, can I buy it somewhere else more cheaply? Some of these decisions will be difficult to make. It is never easy to reduce spending but the freedom of balancing your budget, getting out of debt and giving more generously is well worth the sacrifice. It is important to remember that every spending decision will have an impact on your long-term financial goals.

If, for example, you get rid of satellite television it could save you say £21 a month. If this was invested over five years at a gross interest rate of 10 per cent, you would save £1,626 – enough to pay cash to replace several worn-out appliances. The decision here is do you want more television channels or would you prefer to stay out of debt?

Alternatively, if a family of four eats out once a week and switches to eating out once a month, it could easily save £85 a month. £85 per month invested at 10 per cent would produce over £50,000 in 18 years – enough to pay off the average mortgage years early. You have to ask yourself whether it is better to spend for short-term convenience or save for an important long-term goal.

If someone had debt repayments of £200 a month and was able to increase that payment to £300 a month it is likely they would be out of consumer debt in a relatively short period of time. As soon as the debt repayment was finished they would then have £300 a month to use for current and long-term needs and goals.

Table 3A Joe Bloggs' family budget

Monthly net income	£	£ 1000.00
Formal expenditure		
Mortgage	300.00	
Council tax	45.00	
Electricity	30.00	
Gas	20.00	
Water	20.00	
Telephone	30.00 (E)	
TV licence	8.00 (E)	
Car – MOT, tax, insurance	30.00	
Credit repayments	—	
Household insurance	30.00	513.00
Everday spending		
Food	250.00	
Sundries	50.00	
Childminder	10.00	
Children's pocket money	20.00	
School lunches	30.00	
Toys and books	10.00	
Laundry/dry cleaning	10.00	
Chemist	5.00	
Petrol	50.00	
Parking	10.00	
Public transport	15.00	
TV rental	—	
Video rental	—	
Evening classes	10.00	
Sports/hobbies	20.00	
Tapes and CD's	5.00	
Alcohol	20.00	
Cigarettes/tobacco	—	
Newspapers/magazines	12.00	
Sweets	15.00	
Other	20.00	562.00
Occasional costs		
Christmas	30.00 (E)	
Birthdays	20.00 (E)	
Holidays	40.00 (E)	
Car repairs	20.00 (E)	
House repairs	10.00 (E)	
Redecoration	—	
Vet bills	—	

Clothing	30.00 (E)	
School trips	10.00 (E)	
Dentist	10.00 (E)	
Optician	—	
Meals out	30.00 (E)	
Other	15.00 (E)	215.00

TOTAL EXPENDITURE	**1290.00**

Total income	1000.00	
Total expenditure	1290.00	
Surplus/deficit	(290.00)	

The Bloggs Family is spending £290 a month more than it earns.

Table 3B Adjusting your budget – Joe Bloggs' family (example)

(1) Income increased

Description	Before increase	After increase	Amount increased
Husband – 5 hrs overtime	1,000	1,075.00	75.00
Wife – part-time secretary	Nil	200.00	200.00
Daughter – babysitting	Nil	20.00	20.00
TOTAL INCOME INCREASED			**£295.00**

(2) Spending reduced

Description	Before reduction	After reduction	Amount reduced
Telephone – use off peak	30.00	20.00	10.00
Childminder – halve use of	10.00	5.00	5.00
School lunches – take sandwiches	30.00	10.00	20.00
Petrol – walk to work	50.00	40.00	10.00
Sport – squash just once a week	20.00	10.00	10.00
Alcohol – cut down	20.00	10.00	10.00
Newspapers – stop	12.00	Nil	12.00
Christmas – cut back	30.00	20.00	10.00
Meals out – cut back	30.00	15.00	15.00
TOTAL SPENDING REDUCED			**£102.00**

	Total income increased	295.00
Plus	Total spending reduced	102.00
		397.00
Subtract	(1) Amount needed to balance budget monthly	290.00
	(4) Adjusted surplus or deficit	**£107.00**

Four truths about spending

- The more often we look round the shops the more we will spend.
- The more we watch television the more we will spend.
- The more we look through catalogues the more we will spend.
- The more we read newspapers and magazines the more we will spend.

Remember, it is only possible to make real cuts in your spending by making difficult choices. To help you do this use an 'Adjusting your budget' worksheet (see Tables 3A and 3B) which is designed in four parts:

1 Amount needed to balance your budget
If your estimated budget shows a negative figure enter it into the next to the bottom box. Incidentally, you should do this exercise even if you are already in surplus as it may well show you ways of increasing your giving and savings.

2 Income increased
If there are ways in which your family can regularly increase your income complete this section. Use a separate line for each different way you anticipate doing this.

3 Spending reduced
As you reduce spending complete this section. Again use a new line for each item and subtract the new reduced figure for each item from the old one to see exactly how much you are saving.

4 Study your progress
Add the total increase of income to the reduced spending total and then subtract from this figure the amount needed to balance the budget monthly. If you have a positive figure you are now in surplus. If it is nil you have balanced your budget exactly, but if it is negative you are still spending more than you earn.

Have a look at the example used of balancing the Bloggs' budget (Table 3B) before having a go at balancing your own. Use a pencil and establish priorities until your budget is balanced. Remember it is always easier to do a theoretical exercise for someone else than to do it for real for yourself, but with commitment and patience you will get there.

Preparing a financial statement

There are several good reasons for preparing a financial statement. These include:

- giving you an accurate picture of your money position
- enabling you to see where you can improve your financial position
- having something to show to creditors to convince them about your ability to pay them

For these reasons it is very important when drawing up your statement to:

- be absolutely honest
- look at every category
- involve all members of your family who are old enough to be involved
- keep going over it carefully to make sure you haven't forgotten anything

Do not include any debt repayments in your financial statement. You need to see what surplus you can make available to repay debts before making any offers of repayment.

Assets and liabilities statement

At this stage, particularly if money is still tight, it is a good idea to draw up your family's assets and liabilities statement (see Table 4). You do not need to be precise at this stage – just estimate the amount of each asset and liability. Then ask yourself if there are either assets you no longer require and could sell or liabilities you could reduce. For example, one way of doing this is to move to a smaller house. It is a good idea to review your assets and liabilities statement on a yearly basis to see what significant trends are taking place.

Table 4   **Assets and liabilities statement**
(Estimate as accurately as possible)

Assets (present market value)	£
Home	
Car/motorbike	
Caravan	
Computer	
Furniture	
Consumer goods	
Cash	
Savings	
Shares	
Cash value of life insurance	
Stamps/coins	
Jewellery	
Pension plan	
Other assets	

Liabilities (current amount owed)	£
Mortgage	
Credit arrangements	
Credit cards	
Store cards	
Overdrafts	
Loans	
Personal debts	
Utility debts	
Tax/National insurance	
Other 'secured' loans	
Other 'unsecured' loans	

Net worth (total assets less total liabilities)   £ _____

Often at this stage we may find it hard to sell certain items because they are too important to us. It is here that we need to remind ourselves of the fact that everything we 'own' in fact belongs to God. If you struggle here, I suggest you do what I did. List all your possessions under a heading 'Surrendering to God'. As you make new purchases add them to the list. Keep the list somewhere you can easily find it so that, if you find something is diverting your attention too much, you can get out the list and remind yourself that that item belongs to God. Remember to date the list – the day you surrender all your possessions to Jesus is a day to remember!

Our 'Surrender to God' list looks like this:

On 20 April 1988 we surrender ownership of all our possessions, including the following, to our Lord and Saviour: home, car, domestic appliances, stamp collection, maps, paintings, clothes, furniture, bank account, insurance policy, jobs
December 1991: computer

Signed ....
....
(Stewards of the above)

Why not complete your own list right now?

Steps to ensure your budget works

1 Transfer ownership
What you have just done is the important first step. If you believe that you are the owner of even one possession then the events affecting that possession are bound to affect your attitude. God never forces His will on us, and although it is simple to say that we surrender ownership of everything to God, it is not that easy to do it. That is why drawing up the 'Surrender to God' list helps so much. At first nearly everyone will experience some difficulty in acknowledging God's ownership because we are so

accustomed to self-management and control. But as in all other areas, true financial freedom comes from recognizing that God is in total control.

2 Don't forget 'hidden' bills

These are usually expenses that occur on an annual or irregular basis. Your budget needs to provide for these, or you could suddenly find yourself in trouble if money has not been put aside. An example of a hidden expense is an annual insurance payment. The amount needed should be divided by twelve and set aside every month. Clothing, car repairs, holidays, birthdays, Christmas and other such items should be treated in the same way. Other bills commonly overlooked are annual subscriptions and, for the self-employed, various taxes. On top of these remember that many domestic appliances need replacing over time.

3 Control impulse spending

Impulse items are those things you always see as you are shopping – they are things that you want but do not need. Most major items of impulse spending are bought using credit cards. A survey has indicated that people who use credit cards spend 34 per cent more than people who don't. Impulse spending is a real budget-buster so do everything possible to bring it under control.

4 Plan your present buying

Presents for Christmas and birthdays need to be part of your budget. Think about the total amount you can afford to spend on presents during the year and then make sure to keep to it. Draw up your calendar of birthday and Christmas gifts and allocate the sum of money according to your preferences.

5 Watch miscellaneous spending

I often hear people say, 'I just don't know where the money goes.' Most of it is often categorized as miscellaneous. As you budget your aim is to virtually remove 'miscellaneous' as a category. Determine to see where everything you spend really does go.

6 Accept responsibility in the home
In most families there is only one book-keeper. However, both parties are responsible for the running of the household budget and they need to work out together who does what. Deciding on where money should be spent has to be agreed, especially so that no blame can be attached if anything goes wrong. Husband and wife will not agree on everything, so a fair compromise is needed. Your budget should bring peace into your home where once there was conflict.

7 Develop good records
It is impossible to manage your money without accurate records.

8 Set family goals
It is always much easier to work at something, for example saving for a holiday, if you are all working together.

> When God manages our finances we have nothing to worry about.

Two main areas of expenditure

Housing

Typically this is the largest home budget problem. Many families have bought homes they cannot afford either because of peer pressure or because they believed they would be sharply appreciating investments. Events of the last few years with fluctuating interest rates, job uncertainty and declining house values have hit many people hard. It is not necessary for everyone to own their own home. The decision to buy or rent should be based on needs and financial ability rather than any other pressures.

It should be stated straight away that buying a house without first checking your budget to determine what you can afford will often place a tremendous financial burden on your family. The resulting stress can in fact destroy it. Of course, buying a house within your budget may mean that you have to settle for a smaller house than you would like, but remember the less you owe on your mortgage the quicker you can pay it off. In this way you will be able to help your children through university or plan for your retirement more easily.

Even though your financial situation will be the main factor in determining what type of housing you need there are others that must be considered. Ask yourself the following questions – and answer honestly!

- Do you feel your job is secure enough for you to take on a mortgage? If not consider renting instead of buying.
- Can you easily afford the additional costs, i.e. Council Tax, gas, electricity for the house you are considering buying?
- Do you plan to live in the area for a long time? If you plan to live there for six or more years, then buying may be the best option.
- What is the local economy in the area you are planning to live?
- Are houses appreciating or are there lots for sale?
- Is the cost of living there higher than average?

Borrowing

The Bible does not prohibit borrowing but it does discourage it. Every biblical reference to borrowing is negative. Remember that Proverbs 22.7 (NIV) tells us, 'The rich rule over the poor, and the borrower is servant to the lender.' House owners who lose their jobs and struggle to maintain their mortgage payments soon find out what it is like to be in the position of a slave. Also remember that borrowing is literally a promise to repay and God wants us to keep our promises.

Equity

Another biblical principle that affects us when we borrow is 'surety'. This means taking on obligations to pay at a later date without a sure way of paying them. For example, if you bought a £100,000 home with a £5,000 deposit (equity) then you borrowed £95,000. If the market then drops by more than 5 per cent you will be left in a position where you are owing more than what you can sell the house for. This puts you in an almost impossible position if an emergency occurs and you are forced to sell your property. You have no equity left in the house – in fact after the sale you can owe the mortgage company, or their insurers, a significant sum of money for which they can pursue you for years. However, if you had bought the same house and put down a deposit of £30,000 the market would have to fall enormously before all your equity disappeared.

Negative equity (where your house is worth less than the mortgage on it) has hurt many in this country. It causes frustration, overcrowding (as couples have children they cannot afford to move to larger houses) and relationship breakup. It really is a good idea to save as much as possible before buying. Therefore it is very dangerous to take out a 100 per cent mortgage.

Buying a house

If you have decided to go this route you will first of all have to decide whether you are buying a new or used property. With used houses there are several advantages. You know exactly what the house is going to cost and you often get many extras such as carpets, curtains, light fittings and sometimes some appliances. On the other hand older houses will have some wear and tear and this means repair bills. It is always worth the expense of a survey if you are buying an older house. Problems with the roof, drainage or heating, for example, could be many times the cost of the survey to put right. Alternatively, you could always contemplate buying a run-down house at a knock-down price. You will need to allow extra funds for repairs, so always have the house checked thoroughly, including the foundations, plumbing and wiring, so you know exactly what is wrong with the house before you buy it. If you possess the skills and are able to renovate the house yourself you could make a reasonable profit should you ever wish to sell.

The best way to buy a house is to save up and pay cash for it but in our society this is extremely difficult to do unless you are trading down from a much larger house. Otherwise the best options are:

- Start small.
- Make it as attractive as possible.
- Sell it as house values and your income increases.
- Buy the next sized house.

> Particularly when buying a house, patience is the key.

Mortgages

Most people have a mortgage over 25 years with a rate that fluctuates depending on the government base rate. If rates are relatively low and stable this is fine, but it is important to recognize that in recent years there have been some quite wild swings in interest rates which have put a large number of people under totally unexpected pressure. This has, in fact, led to a sharp increase in the offers of fixed-rate mortgages. These are very helpful from a budgeting point of view because even though they will often have higher interest rates on commencement than flexible loans, you will know exactly what you are paying month after month.

There has also been a big debate in recent years about whether people are better off with endowment or repayment mortgages. A repayment mortgage pays off both capital and interest over the period of the mortgage. An endowment mortgage pays the interest only, but a sum is invested in an endowment policy that matures when the mortgage is due to be repaid and in theory pays off the capital element and also provides a nest egg as well. The rates of growth of most endowments have, however, not been able to be maintained in recent years to the extent that there is a worry that some may not even pay off the mortgage. Given the poor surrender value of these policies in the early years, serious thought needs to be given before taking out this sort of mortgage.

Mortgage insurance

The government has tightened paying out Income Support for mortgage interest. Therefore, it is vital now that comprehensive redundancy and sickness insurance is taken out when taking on a mortgage regardless of the type of mortgage.

Refinancing

If interest rates fall after you buy your house, then you may well be tempted to switch to a cheaper lender. But just because rates are 1 or 2 per cent lower doesn't mean that you should automatically refinance. You need to work out exactly how much in pounds you would actually be saving and then compare it to the costs of switching lenders, which may well include cancellation fees, new title searches and surveys. If these expenses are wiped out over a couple of years then it is probably worth refinancing.

Second mortgages

People often take out second mortgages either for some form of home improvement or simply because they need some more money to pay off their bills. In either case they should be very wary. First, home improvement loans do not usually qualify for benefit payments should you fall on hard times. Second, these are loans secured on your property, and if things go wrong creditors can go to court to repossess. But probably more importantly, you don't need to borrow more money if you can't pay your bills. Borrowing more money, especially against the equity in your house, doesn't actually solve the problem. It only treats a symptom and in a couple of years' time you will probably find yourself in the same situation again. You need to treat the problem itself – so go back to your budget!

Repossessions

In recent years, because of job losses and falling house prices, there has been a steady tide of repossessions – over the last five years 700,000 people have been moved out of repossessed property. If you fall behind on your payments talk to your lender. Make what offer you can afford and try with all your might to stick to it. If it looks like repossession is inevitable try and persuade your lender to let you stay in the property while you try and sell it. You are likely to get a much better price if you do so.

What is important is that you primarily look at the house you are going to buy as a home and not as an investment. It is better to be living in a small, cosy and comfortable house than in a large one with half-empty rooms and high maintenance costs. Most people still owe money on their mortgage when they retire – aim to be an exception.

Renting

If you decide that renting is a better option for you at this time, there are several things to consider. It is always a good idea to ask for help from people in your church. They should be a good source of information about availability, location and price in the surrounding area. Remember when renting that you will have certain extras to pay such as deposit, Council Tax, fuel costs and insurance.

Cars

In our society nearly every family owns at least one car. Most people who are shopping for a car do not need one. They may simply be tired of their old car, it may look old and out of date or it may need repairs to put it back into good condition, or it may simply be that neighbours and/or work colleagues have got newer models. Cars do eventually wear out and have to be replaced, but we often change cars for emotional rather than rational reasons. The advertising media refer to us all as consumers but when buying cars another word is uppermost in their minds. It is the word 'suckers'. Many of us will buy cars we cannot really afford, and trade them in long before their life is over. Those who buy brand new cars, keep them for less than four years and then trade them in for a new model, have usually wasted the largest amounts of money. Some people, such as salespeople, who drive a great deal, need to replace their cars fairly frequently, but nearly all of the rest of us change our cars because we want to, not because we need to. Ego and esteem often cloud our better judgement.

Nearly everyone would like to be sitting behind the wheel of a new car. But we need to ask not only whether we can afford it, but also whether buying a brand new car is the best stewardship of our family's hard-earned money. Costs, including payments, insurance and maintenance for a mid-range new car, frequently exceed £250 a month. That kind of figure can ruin many a family budget. Some may feel they can afford that figure but other items such as food and clothing will invariably suffer, and as these are essential items the family will eventually get into debt to obtain them.

The 'average' family needs to buy a good quality, reliable, used car. Size, style, age and appearance will differ from family to family. If you give in to the temptation to buy a new car, you may be starting a lifetime habit of changing them every few years and losing thousands of pounds each time you drive a new one off the forecourt.

No more than 15 per cent of your net available income should be allocated to motoring expenses. To summarize:

- Honestly evaluate your need for a new car.
- If you need one, it is usually better to buy a good quality used car.
- Look for value (i.e. mileage and condition) as well as price.
- Pay cash whenever possible.
- Check you are getting a good trade-in price for your old car. More often than not you get a better deal if you sell it yourself.

Money saving

Being a good Christian steward also means spending money wisely. This does not mean travelling 40 miles because you have heard that baked beans are 1p cheaper there but it does mean checking around your locality to ensure that you are shopping as economically as possible. When you set your mind to it you can probably think of dozens of ways of doing this. Here are a few ideas to set you on your way.

General

- Only buy on a cash basis. If you cannot afford something try and save up for it.
- Do not be afraid to haggle if you are paying cash.
- When you are thinking of buying something wait for thirty days. Then before you buy it ask yourself if you still need that item. In the meantime check prices.
- Use your washing machine or dishwasher to full potential.
- Buy items out of season. You can always buy Christmas cards half-price in January (as long as you can remember where you put them next December!).
- Learn home and car maintenance.
- Keep budgeting.

Food

- Always use a shopping list.
- Never go shopping when you are hungry.
- Whenever possible avoid taking your children shopping!
- Try own brands.
- Buy long-life food in bulk – as long as you know you will use it.
- Use a calculator to add up the cost as you go along.
- Plan your meals before making your shopping list and buy only for those meals.
- Evaluate whether it is cheaper to buy items such as toothpaste and toiletries from the supermarket or the chemist.
- Avoid as many pre-prepared foods as possible, as you are paying for expensive labour.
- Buy seasonal vegetables when they are cheap.
- Look out for special offers.

Cars

- Establish a repair fund within your budget.
- Keep the car properly maintained.
- Deal with any problems immediately they occur.
- If you are replacing your car look out for:
  - signs of repainting
  - burnt oil on the valves
  - any 'knocking' sounds
  - dirty exhaust
  - any vibration when you brake
  - also check tyres, electricals and carpet and upholstery.

Now it's over to you!

As you get your budget into shape and use your money wisely there are still two things that you need to consider.

Standard of living

The Bible does not prescribe one standard of living for everyone. Each individual's standard of living needs to be worked out carefully with much prayer. You should write down what you and your partner see as your God-given standard of living. Look at the example below:

Karen and Ken's standard of living:

> We are happy living in our present house and have no desire to move to a larger one though we would like to add a conservatory to our home. Our main aims are to see our children through university, clear our mortgage and both give and save an extra 5 per cent each year. Ken wishes to retire at 60 and then work voluntarily for the Church. We intend to change our car every seven years, buying a low-mileage, used car as a replacement. Although we want to remain smart, we do not intend to follow too many fashions. We want to help our children become financially mature but we especially want to put God first in all aspects of our finances.

Now, in discussion with your partner, determine your own standard of living.

The other thing you need to do is:

Determine your financial goals

This will help you to establish what is most important to you financially. It will always give you something to aim at and also help determine whether any major spending decision fits in with your family's priorities. Here is the best way to proceed:

- Complete a financial goals sheet. If you are married it could be sensible initially to produce individual sheets and after comparing the two produce a joint sheet.
- Pray for confirmation of your goals. Just because your present circumstances make them look unlikely do not dismiss them or limit them in any way. Remember, the division of financial responsibilities – our part and God's part. Our part is to do all that we can to be faithful stewards. God's part is to meet our needs and give possessions as He sees fit. Many of your goals may in fact be 'faith' goals that you are trusting God to provide within His timing in the future. It is also important to prioritize your goals. Ask yourselves which are the most important. After all, you do not have to accomplish all your goals at once. Your budget may, for example, not allow you to save for retirement until your children have left home.
- List your goals for the coming year – in this be realistic. It is far better to attain three goals than to become frustrated trying to achieve ten unattainable ones.
- Set a maximum goal. Long term you should have a goal of how much you want to accumulate as a maximum. It is good here to think in terms of provision rather than protection.
- Set a surplus plan. As God moves your financial situation into surplus keep asking Him questions. How much should you give back to the Lord's work? How much does your family need? How much should you save? How much

should you give to your children? (Often as a rationalization for an over–commitment to work, we will buy things for our children instead of spending time with them.)
- Have a look at Charles and Catherine's financial goals (see Table 5) before you start talking about and praying through your own standard of living target and financial goals.

Ask yourself — budgeting

1 Why are we not all called to have the same?
2 How ambitious can I be?
3 Should I feel guilty about my standard of living?
4 Should my living standards rise automatically because my income has increased?
5 How do I make spending decisions?
6 How do I differentiate between needs and wants?
7 What influences me to make certain purchases?

Using credit

We cannot leave this chapter on budgeting without acknowledging that from time to time circumstances may arise when it is necessary to use credit. If you find that you are going to have to purchase something using credit it is vital that you find out what the Annual Percentage Rate of interest is (APR). The APR can vary a great deal and you need to compare these as well as the price to calculate where you can make the best purchase.

Many people claim they use credit cards for convenience and that they are able to obtain from them a few weeks' interest-free credit. But beware. About half of all credit card holders do not pay off their balance in full each month and, as indicated, surveys show that people who own credit cards tend to spend significantly more than similar income-earners who do not use them. Debit cards, such as Switch, are just as convenient and user-friendly, but help discipline you to keep within your spending limits. You are also likely to think twice before spending when you know that your money will be debited from your bank straight away!

Table 5   **Financial goals** (example)

Names: Charles and Catherine
Date: 1.1.96

Giving goals
We would like to give 15 per cent of our income.
Other giving goals:
To sponsor one needy child
To help support a missionary regularly
To give to a Christian charity that helps mentally handicapped people.

Debt repayment goals
We would like to reduce or pay off the following debts:
    1. Car loan   £2,000
    2. Credit card   £700
    3. Store card   £500
We would also like to reduce our mortgage by making 13 payments this
year and we will not take out any new credit commitments.

Educational goals
We would like to set aside money for our child's education

Person	College	Annual cost	Total cost
Mike	University	£1,500	£5,000
	(to be decided)		

Lifestyle goals
We would like to make the following purchases:
    Double-glaze front door   £600
    Get new refrigerator   £300
We would like jointly to achieve the following annual income: £25,000

Savings goals
We would like to save 7.5 per cent of our income.
Other savings goals: to increase this to 10 per cent within the next five years.

We would like to make the following investments:
    Retirement Plan   £1,500 per year
We would also like to provide our children with the following when we die:
Home paid for and cash gifts of £5,000 each.

Business goals:
We would like to begin our own business. Not applicable.

Goals for this year
We believe that God wants us to achieve the following goals this year:

Priority	Financial goals	Our part	God's part
1	Increase giving	Write cheque after analysing/praying where to give	Provide money and direction
2	Balance budget	Reduce spending	Give wisdom
3	Pay off car loan	Sell car	Provide buyer

Ask yourself – credit

1 Am I as aware as I should be of the various forms of credit available?
2 What is roughly the lowest rate of interest and where would I find it?
3 Who charges really high rates of interest?
4 Would I have a problem with my credit commitments if I lost my job?
5 How influenced am I by the advertising/mail I get offering me credit deals?
6 Is there ever such a thing as interest-free credit?
7 Does the widespread availability of credit increase my desire for possessions?

3 DEBT

Introduction

Although this chapter gives a general overview, debt can be a highly complex subject and if you have debt problems you should take expert advice straight away. Go to a Money Advice Unit, Citizens' Advice Bureau or ring Credit Action's freephone debt helpline on 0800 591084. They can provide a variety of material that can specifically help you.

> Plaque in a gift shop – 'Money talks – and mine just said goodbye!'

People who are in financial bondage are preoccupied with money, worried about how they will meet their current obligations or are constantly driven to strive for more. Most will be in debt and also have poor spending habits. They will be behind in paying bills, be unable to save and feel discontented. Because of this they do not have the financial freedom which would allow them to make their own decisions regarding money. Current circumstances and the attitudes of their creditors dictate where the money goes.

Over the past 20 years the incidence of debt has reached epic proportions in our society. It has had an impact on nearly everybody and sadly the Christian experience is little different. Many Christians today are shackled by excessive debts, and this misuse of their finances can often ruin their spiritual lives. They often are no longer able to minister to people as God directs. They feel weighed down and have a timidity in speaking about Jesus because the freedom that He brings is not marked in their lives. Until we learn to make sacrifices and cut out much impulse spending, we will remain in financial slavery. We will never experience true peace of mind until we have our debt firmly under control.

One of the things that has happened over this recent period is that the negative concept of 'debt' has been cleverly replaced by the positive picture of 'credit'. We are encouraged to think of ourselves as respectable citizens who could surely do with just a little more credit to help us on our way. With society screaming at us that if we want something we should go for it straight away, there is little wonder that many of us succumb to the pressure. Since 1979 the amount of money owing in Britain on personal mortgages, credit and store cards has multiplied twenty times. There is also a personal cost. The number of children in families on Income Support currently stands at around three million. This is three times the number for 1979. In fact, there is so much debt in this country that Mr Average has been described as someone driving on a government bond-financed road, in a bank-financed car, fuelled by credit card-financed petrol, going to buy store card-financed furniture to put in his mortgage-financed house!

Now all this may seem to be all right when things are going well, but if the unexpected happens debt can have devastating consequences. One of the biggest problems in our rapidly changing society is that these days you can also expect the unexpected to happen. Mortgages still normally last 25 years. How many people have a job for as long as that? Sadly, it is my belief that most people who leave school or university today will face redundancy at least once in their lifetime. If they are over-committed financially when this happens they could hit real trouble very quickly. As the world becomes increasingly one global market this too can place increasingly volatile pressures on workers. For example, even now the phone bill you receive every quarter is printed in India because with modern technology it is cheaper to use satellites and a lower paid workforce. Quite what the long-term implications for this sort of transaction are is hard to fathom. It could be argued that anything that brings jobs and stability to a Third World country is a good thing. But it will inevitably have ramifications for the levels of unemployment in this country. Already approximately four million court summonses are issued for debt in Britain each year and at any one time there are more people in prison for unpaid fines than for any other reason.

The impact and effects of debt

In a society where success is usually gauged by what sort of house we live in and how much we earn, debt can so often be linked with failure. We even ask people when we meet them for the first time, 'What do you do?' as if somehow we should value them more highly if they have an important job. Thankfully God does not value us like this. He looks at our heart, our love for Jesus, our compassion for others and our desire to reach the lost. I pray constantly for the same value system in my own life.

But we are commonly so afraid of money that when something goes wrong we try and hide that there is a problem. Unemployment, loss of overtime or commission can be a major cause of income taking a tumble and certainly these have been major factors in recent years. Other have tried to work on a self-employed basis but found it very hard to succeed. But there are other factors as well. The reduction in student grants and the encouragement of loans is beginning to have quite an impact on many young people as they start their careers several thousands of pounds in debt. But other factors can include sickness or injury, a significant change in circumstances, such as a new baby, relationship breakdown, lack of awareness of the benefit system, changes in interest rates or trying too hard to 'keep up with the Joneses'. It can be seen that many of these factors are outside most people's control – and it is precisely these feelings of helplessness that cause so much despair.

Debt brings a wide range of different emotions. Perhaps the most overwhelming one is that of fear. You may be afraid to open the post, knowing it is likely to contain further bills. Every time the door bell or the phone rings you fear that it may be the bailiffs or another angry creditor. You may well be afraid of talking to your partner about the situation. You may be afraid of facing up to the whole picture yourself. But there are other feelings too. You will probably feel uneasy and insecure. You may well feel guilty. It could be that you feel guilty because if you had been nicer to the boss he might not have sacked you. It is more likely, however, that you feel guilty because you realize that in the recent past you have been spending money on things you haven't really needed and now you are going to struggle to buy essentials.

Other feelings include loneliness. Debt often makes people withdraw. It could be that you don't want to keep seeing people who constantly remind you of the 'good old days' before things went wrong. But often it is even simpler than that. You may no longer go out with friends because you can no longer afford to pay your share. And people can feel very depressed – dreams that had been cherished for years of that special home, car or holiday can lie in ruins as the reality of debt hits home.

And the effects of debt are devastating. Relate has named it as the major cause of relationship breakdown in over 70 per cent of cases. The NSPCC has stated that money problems are a major cause of family pressure which can lead to child abuse. Many will try and bottle up their problems and pretend there are no troubles, the commonplace 'I'm fine' covering up the anguish that is really being felt. As a result many health problems occur due to the pressure and stress. People also lose their self-esteem. Sadly, for a few life no longer seems worth living. The first time I ever spoke at a Christian gathering someone came up to me afterwards in tears. He said he was so pleased that these sorts of issues were at last being addressed by the Church. The previous Saturday they had been due to go out with friends, but these friends had rung to say that their 27-year-old daughter had killed herself because of money worries. The last place she had turned to for help had been her local church, but they had said there was nothing they could do to help.

Debt is a big issue. It is also largely a hidden problem but it can have devastating consequences. Time and time again you can read of assaults, marriage breakdown, robberies and even murder, and find that the cause has been debt. You cannot tell by appearances who it will hit or where. After I had spoken at a church fairly recently the pastor commented that he was glad I had preached on money in general rather than debt, because they lived in an affluent part of the country where debt wasn't a problem. I learned later that 47 copies of the book *Escape from Debt* had been sold after the service!

After I had spoken at a church in London a very well-dressed lady came over to speak to me and said that debt was a subject in which she had a particular interest. She went on to tell me that six months previously her husband had killed himself the day before their house was due to be repossessed. He was a doctor and nobody knew he had any financial problems. In fact, one of the elders in her church told me later, if they had conducted a survey within the church to name the wealthiest person, most people would have assumed it was her husband. Debt is no respecter of persons. In recent years many accountants, estate agents, solicitors and other professional classes have been hit hard by recession, unemployment and falling house prices. In fact, in percentage terms, more of these groupings have had their houses repossessed than those on lower incomes. Traditionally, these have been recession-proof professions and therefore the shock can be even greater for them.

Credit reference agencies

Another reason for trying to avoid debt is that almost everyone will be on file with one of the credit reference agencies. If we have County Court judgements against us or have even been slow payers it could mean that we may be turned down for credit for up to six years from the time concerned. If you are turned down for credit and don't know why, seek advice from Credit Action or another money advice agency which will explain what to do next.

Debt — the barriers

There are many reasons why people are reluctant to talk about money issues. First, it is a taboo subject for many. Second, as I have said, many people gauge how successful you are by how much you have – so to admit to being in debt is akin to saying you are a second-class citizen. But then there are other fears too – fears of your ignorance of money matters surfacing, fears of someone (probably your partner) saying 'I told you so'. Fears that you will worry your partner, that others will reject you when they find out the truth. Fear of losing face.

The difference between having debts and being in debt

I believe that life in the West is virtually impossible without some form of borrowing – particularly if a house is being purchased. A mortgage is a debt because you are obliged to pay it until it is paid off, usually over 25 years. However, you are not in debt until you miss a payment that should have been made. As Christians we should do all in our power to let no debt remain outstanding when it should have been paid.

The dictionary defines debt as 'money or property which one person is obligated to pay to another'. Therefore, this includes money owed to building societies, banks, credit and store card companies as well as friends and relatives. A bill which is due (e.g. an electricity bill) would not be considered a debt if it is paid on time. On this basis our Christian responsibility is to ensure that any borrowing is sensible and does not undermine our financial responsibility and thus thwart our aims of being faithful stewards of God's money. Before we borrow money for any purpose we should consider all the circumstances and seek wisdom from others who can help us evaluate all aspects of the decision, including the risks involved.

What to do when borrowing

There are several things to consider before borrowing.

Evaluate all the options carefully – look at the level of interest rates, any penalty clauses and levels of repayment. Remember that when you borrow, compound interest is working against you. Over the life of a typical mortgage you are likely to pay back over three times the amount you borrowed. But the problems are even more acute with credit and store cards where interest rates can be in excess of 30 per cent per annum. If you do not pay the amount you owe in full every month, and about half of us in this country don't, then interest just accumulates on interest. It is so easy to slip into debt for this reason and so much harder to get out of it.

Then ensure you have the money available to repay the loan. Ask yourself questions such as, Can I easily afford this? Are there any cheaper options? Could I afford the repayments if interest rates rose sharply? What happens if I lose my job or become ill? Are these loans insurable? Then, and only then, if you are happy with your answers, take out the loans and make the repayments on time.

Avoiding irresponsible decisions

I believe there are several guidelines which we need to follow to avoid making poor financial decisions. These include:

- We must never borrow money to buy things which glorify us and not God (Matthew 6.3–4).
- We are not to buy things for materialistic reasons – our treasures should not be on earth (Matthew 6.24).
- We must never be dishonest (1 Timothy 6.10).
- We must never borrow money and use it for ungodly purposes (Romans 12.1–2).

If borrowing money means we will be unable to give God the 'first fruits' of our income we should not take on the loan. If we are already in this position we need to confess that we have done wrong and accept forgiveness (1 John 1.9). We should then draw up a plan to enable us to clear our debts and start trying to make personal sacrifices so that we are able to start giving, if only a small amount initially.

What the Bible says about debt

The Bible's position on debt is clear. Romans 13.8 says, 'Let no debt remain outstanding' (NIV). There are other points that the Bible makes too:

Debt equates to slavery

When we read Proverbs 22.7 we realize why God speaks so directly against debt: 'The borrower is servant to the lender' (NIV). The deeper we are in debt the more we become subject to the demands of the people to whom we owe money. We no longer have the freedom to decide where to spend our income. In 1 Corinthians 7.23 Paul writes, 'You were bought at a price; do not become slaves of men' (NIV). Our Heavenly Father made the ultimate sacrifice for us. He now wants His children to be free to serve Him in the way He chooses. Over the years I must have had dozens of Christians come to me, many of them in tears, because they felt so trapped by their debts that they were unable to live as God intended for them. Debt can shackle your giving, your ministry and your spiritual growth.

Debt was considered a punishment for disobedience

In the Old Testament being debt-free was one of the promised rewards for obedience. 'All these blessings will come upon you and accompany you if you obey the Lord your God . . . You will lend to many nations but will borrow from none' (Deuteronomy 28.2, 12 NIV). Equally, later on in the same chapter indebtedness was one of the punishments inflicted for disobedience. 'The alien who lives among you will rise above you higher and higher, but you will sink lower and lower. He will lend to you, but you will not lend to him. He will be the head, but you will be the tail' (Deuteronomy 28. 43–4 NIV).

Debt makes assumptions about tomorrow

Whenever you take on a debt you are making the assumption that you will be able to repay it out of your future income. God may well have different plans for you! The Bible warns us clearly not to assume such things.

> Now listen, you who say, 'Today or tomorrow we will go to this or that city, spend a year there, carry on business and

make money.' Why, you do not even know what will happen tomorrow. What is your life? You are a mist that appears for a little while and then vanishes. Instead, you ought to say, 'If it is the Lord's will we will live and do this or that.' (James 4.13–15 NIV)

Debt may deny God

Rather than rushing into debt to buy the latest domestic appliance you should always pray about it first. God may well put it into someone's heart to give you what you need. What a blessing it is when both giver and receiver hear God's voice.

Can Christians ever borrow money?

The Bible does not specifically answer this question, but using biblical principles it would seem it is acceptable to borrow in the following circumstances:

- The item purchased is likely to increase in value over time.
- The value of the item being purchased significantly exceeds the amount being borrowed (this is called equity).
- The repayments put no strain on your budget.

A small mortgage would fit these criteria. Historically a house has been an appreciating asset. The pressures come when people have either paid too high a price or have over-borrowed. In recent years when prices stagnated many were caught in the negative equity trap and the strains this can cause cannot be overstated. The problem today is that many young couples will take on far too much borrowing too quickly. Not only will they take out a significant mortgage but they will also have loans for car, carpets and domestic appliances. They may well still have student loans outstanding as well.

How to get out of debt

I believe that debt-free living is still God's plan for us today. The blessings of becoming debt-free go beyond the financial area.

Money problems inevitably spill over into prayer and quiet times. They also invariably have an adverse impact on marriage relationships. Because of this the first thing you need to do before establishing a plan to get out of debt is to look at your attitudes. Do you feel financially competent? Sadly, many of us have never been taught how to manage money. Our society is no help – its philosophy is 'Spend, spend, spend. Even if you can't afford it you should get it anyway because you deserve it.' This attitude leads to indulgence as we think we need everything now. The whole concept of starting out small and gradually building a step at a time has all but disappeared. This is a symptom of poor planning. Anyone who tries to live without a plan showing income and expenditure is on the road to potential financial disaster.

A plan to get out of debt

Financial freedom will show itself in every aspect of our lives. When God manages our finances we have nothing to worry about. Here are the steps to give us the financial freedom we all long for:

Pray
In 2 Kings 4.1–7 a widow was threatened with losing her children to a creditor and so she appealed to Elisha for help. Elisha told her to borrow as many empty jars from her neighbours as she could. Then God supernaturally multiplied her only possession – a small amount of oil – until all the jars were filled. By selling the oil she was able to pay off her debt and keep her children. God wants us to be debt-free as well. The first and most important step is to pray. He may act straight away or over time but He will multiply our efforts to get out of debt.

Transfer ownership
As has previously been said, true financial freedom can only come by transferring ownership of everything to God.

Establish a budget
Very few people use a written budget, yet it should be an

absolute essential for everyone. Refer to chapter 2 on budgeting, and ensure that you have trimmed your expenditure as much as you can.

Look at your list of assets
Is there anything that can be sold to reduce or eliminate your debts?

Look at your list of liabilities
Many of us, if we owe substantial sums of money, do not know the full extent of our debts. Although it is natural to want to hide from unpleasant things, it is only when we look at the true picture that we can take steps to rectify the situation.

Establish a debt repayment schedule
You need to produce a plan to repay all your creditors. If this is your situation I would strongly recommend you obtain a self-help guide for people who are in debt. However, as a general guide you need to pay your priority debts first. Priority debts are those where you stand to lose things if you don't pay, i.e., you could lose your home if you don't pay your mortgage or you could be cut off if you don't pay your gas, electricity or water bills.

Seek ways of obtaining additional income
It is always worth exploring ways of earning extra income but do not do this at the expense of your relationship with God and your family. If you can earn more, use that money to pay off your debts.

Do not accumulate new debt
The only way of doing this is to use cash, cheque or debit cards. Statistics show that people spend more when they use credit cards because they feel they are not really spending money – it is only when the bill arrives that it hits home! So especially if you are in debt because of the misuse of credit, stop using credit cards altogether. It is essential that you learn to sacrifice some wants and desires if you are to get out of financial bondage.

Learn to be content with what you have

We live in a society where advertising constantly induces us to buy. Often the message is meant to make us feel dissatisfied with what we already have. So a Christian in debt should resolve to stop spending on anything which is non-essential. Each one of us needs to learn to live on what God provides and not be driven by the desire for material things.

Consider a change of lifestyle

By slightly lowering your standard of living you can usually get out of debt more quickly. Is it possible to have a smaller home or car? In the light of the needs around us this is something we should all be considering.

Practise saving

Even if it is only saving £5 a month we should learn the discipline of saving. This does not mean storing up large sums of money whilst failing to pay your creditors but it is a good sign that you are beginning to get your finances under control.

Maintain your giving

If a sacrifice is necessary, and it almost certainly is, do not sacrifice either God's or your creditors' share. In the light of eternity try and make sacrifices in your expenditure.

Put others first

Make sure you do not benefit at the expense of someone else. Even if in debt yourself show understanding to those who owe money to you. All of us need to be gracious to people who have borrowed money with good intentions and then have faced crises beyond their control which have made it difficult for them to make their loan repayments on time.

Balance your time

If you are having to work every waking moment to try and prevent your debt situation from deteriorating, then there is something wrong. Your priorities are God and your family, so try and strike a sensible balance.

Seek Christian counselling
Whenever in doubt seek good Christian counselling. Many of us do not have the necessary knowledge to handle our money as God intends, so we are likely just to give up. But God has provided others to help.

Do not give up
There are basically three elements to getting out of debt and they are all hard. First you must stop spending more than you earn. Second, the interest on debt has to be paid and, last, you have to pay back what you have borrowed. It is never easy to get out of debt but the freedom is well worth the struggle.

As you study this plan be realistic. Think of the best course of action to take for your future. Be realistic about your facts, think constructively and concentrate on ensuring that your future financial picture will look brighter than the past.

Debt repayment responsibilities

It is not biblical to delay paying bills until the last possible moment. Proverbs 3.28 says: 'Do not say to your neighbour, "Come back later; I'll give it tomorrow"– when you now have it with you' (NIV). We should pay all our bills as promptly as we can whilst at the same time maintaining a reasonable level of savings to act as a cushion should future emergencies occur.

Practical help – debt list
As I have said earlier, many people do not know exactly what they owe. The debt list (see Table 6) will help you see not only the list of debts but also the terms of each of them. The seven columns on the list are:

1 the creditor to whom the money is owed
2 the item purchased with the money borrowed
3 the amount of each monthly payment
4 the amount of the outstanding balance

5 the date (where applicable) by which the debt will be fully paid
6 the rate of interest being charged for the debt
7 the number of overdue payments, if any

Table 6 **Debt list** (example)

Arthur and Ethel Blank
Date: 1 January 1996

Creditor	What purchased	Monthly repay-ments	Balance due	Scheduled pay off date	Interest rate	Payments outstand-ing
Smiths' store	Various items	£20	£400	Forever	25%	Nil
Credit card co.	Various items	£30	£600	Forever	22%	Nil
Another credit card co.	Various items	£20	£500	Forever	20%	Nil
John's cars	Car	£150	£5,000	12/99	20%	3
Happy bank loan	Extension	£100	£2,000	12/97	18%	3
Bank overdraft	Various items	£50	£600	No date	13%	Nil
Family	Holiday	?	£1,200	No date	Nil	Nil
SUB TOTAL		**£370**	**£5,800**			
Mortgage friendly building society	House	£330	£30,000	Feb 2011	9%	3
Business debt	Nil					
TOTAL DEBTS		**£700**	**£35,800**			

After entering each debt, add up the monthly repayments, balance due and outstanding arrears columns for future reference.

Have a look at the example of Arthur and Ethel Blank in Table 6 before producing your own.

Assume that after working out their revised budget the Blanks had a surplus of £120 a month to pay off their debts. Their debt repayment schedule could then look like Table 7.

Table 7

Debt	Amount outstanding	Extra monthly repayments
Mortgage	990	90
Extension loan (unsecured)	300	12
Car loan	450	18
	1,740	120

The Blanks would be trying to get their mortgage up to date quickly as it is a priority debt. The other unsecured debts can be paid off on a pro rata basis.

After eleven months the situation would look like Table 8.

Table 8

Debt	Amount outstanding	Extra monthly repayments
Extension loan	168	48
Car loan	252	72
	420	120

It can be seen from Table 8 that the total debts will be paid off in a further three and a half months. At this stage it would be good to use the £120 a month to reduce and eventually clear all credit and store card balances which, although within limits, are an expensive way of borrowing.

Debt repayment schedule

The next step is to complete a debt repayment schedule for each outstanding debt. This should help you get out of debt systematically. First complete the information required at the top of the schedule and then follow the four columns:

1 the date each payment is due
2 the amount of each monthly payment
3 the number of payments remaining
4 the loan balance due after each payment (To enable you to complete this accurately you will need regular statements from your creditor.)

Have a look at the example shown in Table 9 before starting any of your own schedules.

Bankruptcy

In certain extreme cases where someone has little or no assets and substantial liabilities they may be tempted to go bankrupt. The Bible tells us that 'the wicked borrow and do not repay' which seems to rule out bankruptcy as an option for Christians. However, if emotional pressures and/or unreasonable behaviour of creditors are causing unbearable stress, then I believe there are times when it can be justified. Of course, a creditor can make someone bankrupt in any case. It is my belief that if this happens Christians should still try and repay their debts if circumstances improve significantly in the future enabling them to do so. I believe this should be the case even if they have been discharged from bankruptcy.

Acting as guarantor

Anyone who acts as a guarantor is legally becoming responsible for the potential debts of another. Proverbs 17.18 tells us, 'A man lacking in judgement strikes hands in pledge' (NIV). Acting as guarantor is not sensible so don't do it!

Table 9   **Debt repayment schedule** (example)

Date:	January 1996		
Creditor:	Happy bank		
Purchase:	Extension		
Amount owed:	£2,000	Interest rate: 18%	

Date due	Payment amount	Payments remaining	Balance due (£)
15 Jan	100	23	1,930.00
15 Feb	100	22	1,858.93
15 Mar	100	21	1,786.83
15 Apr	100	20	1,713.63
15 May	100	19	1,630.33
15 June	100	18	1,563.92
15 July	100	17	1,487.38
15 Aug	100	16	1,409.69
15 Sept	100	15	1,330.84
15 Oct	100	14	1,250.80
15 Nov	100	13	1,169.56
15 Dec	100	12	1,087.10
15 Jan	100	11	1,003.41
15 Feb	100	10	918.46
15 Mar	100	9	832.24
15 Apr	100	8	744.72
15 May	100	7	655.89
15 June	100	6	565.73
15 July	100	5	474.22
15 Aug	100	4	381.33
15 Sept	100	3	287.05
15 Oct	100	2	191.36
15 Nov	100	1	94.23
15 Dec	100	—	—

Where to go for help

God

Always turn to the Lord first. Remember how God sees you. He doesn't care about how much you earn. He doesn't ask 'What do you do?' He looks at your heart, your love for His Son and your compassion for others. You have real hope. An eternal hope but also a practical hope for now. God made you and is with you. He loves you and has plans for you and He hears your cries for help.

Two verses that I personally have found very helpful when facing difficulty are '"For I know the plans I have for you," declares the Lord, "plans to prosper you and not to harm you, plans to give you hope and a future"' (Jeremiah 29.11 NIV), and 'Cast *all* your anxiety on him because he cares for you' (1 Peter 5.7 NIV).

I know of a family who a decade or so ago seemed to have everything – big house, cars, a luxurious lifestyle – but it was all a sham. One day the wife looked into a cupboard she normally didn't use because she couldn't reach it and found nearly a year's unopened post. Within months they were bankrupt and at their lowest point they cried out for help and Christ answered their call. They now live in a small rented cottage with next to nothing materially, but they have time and love for others in abundance and they have led many others to follow Christ. Whatever your situation Jesus is there now, arms outstretched ready to hold and protect you.

Christian advisers

Often when I am counselling people with money problems I come to the conclusion that virtually all their financial difficulties could have been avoided if they had sought advice *before* making the decisions that helped get them into such a desperate situation. The cost can be so much more than financial. We usually do not seek help because we are too proud – looking to others is seen as a sign of weakness. Proverbs 11.2 tells us, 'When pride comes, then comes disgrace' (NIV). We are also stubborn. We believe we are right and often we don't want to hear the true facts because our minds are already made up. We have already set our heart on that beautiful new car and we certainly don't want to be told we cannot afford it. 'The way of the fool is right to him, but a wise man listens to advice' (Proverbs 12.15 NIV). More details about seeking advice can be found later on in this chapter.

Your local Benefits Agency

Many people are not claiming benefits to which they are entitled. Go along to your local Benefits Agency and ask them which benefits you are able to claim.

Your creditors

It is vital that you write to all your creditors and let them know what is happening. If some adverse circumstances have taken place in your life let them know – they cannot be sympathetic to your cause if they don't know what it is.

Your doctor

If you have been under stress because of your money worries and you feel your health is suffering, go and talk to your doctor.

Local support groups

If there are groups in your area, consider joining. The sharing of experiences and the realization that you are not alone will bring huge benefits.

Money advice groups

There should be such a group in your area run by either your local authority, Citizens' Advice Bureau or Money Advice Centre. In some areas there are Christian organizations which offer debt counselling, as well as Christian solicitors and insolvency practitioners who can also help.

What can the Church do to help those with debt problems?

The first thing to do is acknowledge that every community and probably every church has people who are in debt. The first print run of my book *Escape from Debt* sold out in eight weeks! I also know of a church that wrote to every house in their community saying they thought debt was a problem in their area and that there was a new Christian book available to help people in debt. They offered free copies of the book to anyone who wanted it and they received 150 replies! People apparently said things like, 'I didn't know the Church spoke my language.' Money has an impact upon everybody and therefore presents a great outreach opportunity.

The next thing the Church must do is *raise awareness of the problem*. Because so many people keep quiet about their problems those in debt often feel isolated and alone. One of the most amazing experiences of my life so far took place when I had preached at an informal evening service in a Midlands city. After I had spoken the minister said he would like to ask the first question which was, 'Do you really believe debt is a problem here in what is an affluent part of the city?' Looking at the number of people in the church my reply was simply in the affirmative. The minister then said he found this very hard to believe, but at that moment a lady actually stood up and said, 'I'm sorry but you don't know your congregation very well.' At this point I must admit to expecting to see the minister retire gracefully, but instead he immediately shot himself in the other foot! 'I haven't seen you around for some time, Daisy,' he said, to which she replied, 'No you haven't, but as you know John and I had a little boy about a year ago and then a few months ago John lost his job. We found we were in quite substantial debt and we started arguing and arguing and eventually things got so bad I took my baby back to my mum's three months ago. The reason I haven't been to church recently is because I haven't been able to afford the bus fare and the reason that both John and I are here tonight is because we believe it is our last chance of saving our marriage.'

A stunned silence filled the church and then the most wonderful thing happened. A group of normally reserved British Christians suddenly became the Body of Christ. Some were on their knees in prayer and others were in tears. Both husband and wife were engulfed in hugs and others were sitting quietly with their cheque books open. I watched the Body of Christ – refreshing, restoring, giving hope – and then I went home because I was no longer needed.

It is important to *ensure counselling is available.* Some churches can, and have, set up very successful counselling centres. But not all have the resources. Nevertheless they should at least have the local and national phone numbers and addresses of money advice agencies. These could be pinned on the noticeboard where they are easily accessible so as to avoid any embarrassment.

I will never forget the phone call I received one day from an accountant. He completely broke down on the phone and it was some time before he was able to tell me that he had run up huge debts and did not know where to turn. His church had been unable to help. Eventually I asked him if I could talk with his wife but he said, 'You haven't fully understood. I'm not at home, I've been driving around for the last three days and I'm miles away from home.' When I rang his wife she was beside herself with worry as she thought he might have committed suicide. It took a day of phone calls to finally reunite them with each other.

It is also very useful to *have a fund available for those in real immediate need* which is easily and quickly accessible. At Spring Harvest several years ago a young mum came to see me. It was obvious just from looking at her that she was deeply distressed. Married with two small children, her husband had been out of work for a long time and they had lived on benefits. Then he got a job and it boosted his self-esteem so much she did not want to deflate him by telling him that she did not have enough to pay the rent and buy food. She had decided it was more important to buy food and had stopped paying the rent. Every day she expected to hear from the landlord. The rent became an obsession. She went to the church and asked for a loan but they were unable to help. She went to the doctor and was prescribed tranquillizers. Eventually, after four months, she received a letter from the landlord and went to see him. The landlord offered a way out and in desperation she went to bed with him to 'pay off the debt'. She told me she had been unable to look in the mirror since. I talked to her of God's forgiveness and prayed that her husband would be able to forgive too. The saddest thing of all was that their income was in fact so low that they were entitled to benefits which would have paid the rent in full.

Remember the church often sees the tip of the iceberg. There are currently 27,000 debt collectors visiting three million borrowers every week. Some have been charging up to 1,000 per cent interest legally. These figures do *not* include the loan sharks who are operating illegally. Debt, particularly if money-lenders are involved, can become very nasty. In my own home town recently someone who owed £200 to money-lenders and was unable to pay on the due day had his house smashed up very badly and his two dogs were blinded and had to be put down. Many single parents and unemployed people will be in debt, and because they are turned down by reputable lenders such as building societies they have to resort to money-lenders. Many will not admit that they are in debt but we need desperately in our churches to create an atmosphere of trust where people can be open without fear of judgement or gossip.

I spoke fairly recently at one of the biggest churches in the country. Afterwards a very smartly dressed lady came to see me and told me she had lost her job several months ago. I went through her outgoings and then asked about her income. She said that she'd already told me she didn't have a job. When I asked her about benefits she told me that she thought they were for poor people and added that she thought she was supposed to trust God to supply her needs. I gently asked if I could look in her purse. 'There's no point,' she replied, 'there's nothing in it.' I carried on, 'When did you last eat?' She told me that a friend had bought her a doughnut three days ago. I was horrified, but God often has a way of humbling us. Not two weeks later I became aware of a similar situation with someone with whom I was on nodding acquaintance in my own church.

Whenever possible we need to give *practical help*. For example, some people who have been made redundant may have lost their car. We can arrange lifts to school, the supermarket, wherever. It is vital that we *restore dignity*. Show people that you value them for themselves and not for their job, status or financial position. Remember that God wants to work through us so we should *make ourselves available* to those in need. *Be vulnerable* so that others feel they can open up to us and *do not be judgemental*. In short we need to *be like Jesus*.

The need for good advice

The reason that someone seeks advice is to secure insights, hear suggestions and look at alternatives so that they can have a more complete picture before a decision is reached. After gathering all the relevant information and ideas it is important to submit all to God so that He can bring you peace of mind on the decision you take. You can take advice from the following sources.

The Bible

It is obvious that this should be a major source of advice. Psalm 119.98–100 tells us, 'Your commands make me wiser than my enemies, for they are ever with me. I have more insight than all my teachers, for I meditate on your statutes. I have more understanding than the elders, for I obey your precepts' (NIV). God uses the Bible to communicate His truth. Remember the Bible contains over 2,350 verses on handling money so it's a good place to start! If it clearly answers the question posed then there is really no need to go any further because the Bible shows God's revealed will.

Godly people

If the Bible is not specific about a particular issue, seek out people with mature godly wisdom. Christians need each other. Psalm 37.30–31 tells us, 'The mouth of the righteous man utters wisdom, and his tongue speaks what is just. The law of his God is in his heart; his feet do not slip' (NIV).

Husbands or wives

If we are married the first person from whom we should seek advice is our partner. A major financial decision should be agreed upon together as both will experience the consequences of that decision. In doing this you prevent the possibility of a later 'I told you so' response. It also raises your partner's self-esteem because you are actually saying that you really value his or her opinion. You are keeping your partner up to date with your financial situation. The number of people I have counselled who have failed to seek their partner's advice or, worse still, haven't even told them about the real financial situation is considerable. Often the motive appears reasonable – 'I didn't want to worry her' – but in reality we are called to be together for better or for worse. Furthermore it is inevitable that one's partner will eventually find out the truth and when they do they are most likely to be hurt and angry about the breakdown in trust rather than anything else.

Parents

Our parents have seen us grow up and they know our strengths and weaknesses. They also have our best interests at heart. They will be pleased that you have asked for their opinion, but the advice of your parents should always be secondary to the advice of your partner.

Expert advice

Never be afraid of asking for expert help. I would never buy a car without first seeking the advice of my friend who is a car mechanic. Debt is a very complicated and emotive subject. Please seek expert advice at the first opportunity.

Several counsellors

If we have to take a particularly difficult decision we may need to seek the advice of several people. The recommendations may not always be the same, but sometimes a common theme will appear, or each counsellor may provide a missing piece of the jigsaw.

God

Of course, God is the most important source of advice. In Isaiah 9.6 He is called 'Wonderful Counsellor' and in Psalm 32.8 He promises, 'I will instruct you and teach you in the way you should go; I will counsel you and watch over you' (NIV). Whenever we feel uncertain or confused we need to find a quiet place where we can wait to hear His still, small voice.

Avoid bad advice

Never seek help from fortune-tellers or the stars. Also be on your guard against biased advice. Ask yourself if the person giving the advice stands to gain or lose from your decision.

If you are seeking advice:

- Tell the person concerned *all* the relevant facts.
- Never try and manipulate the 'facts' to get the advice you would like to hear.
- Always spend time reading the Bible and seeking God.
- Be selective in your choice of counsellors – they should have the courage to oppose your views if they honestly believe that to be the more godly way and/or because it would be in your best interests to do so.
- Remember that good interaction with others can often lead to the right path becoming clear to you.

Ask yourself

1 Am I now aware of the most common emotions debt can cause?
2 Am I aware of the consequences of debt?
3 Why do I think so many people find it hard to talk about their financial difficulties?
4 When I make a purchase do I assess whether it is a need, want or desire?
5 Do I always ensure what I purchase is the best possible buy I can get?
6 Do I always pay back what I owe and on time?
7 Have materialism and consumerism had too great an effect on my life?
8 If in debt, have I resolved to do all that is necessary to get out of it as quickly as possible?

4 GIVING

I believe that giving is about the most frustrating aspect of Christian living. Usually the main reason for this is that there is a lack of understanding about what the Bible actually teaches. In particular, there seems often to be an attitude of 'Well, as we're no longer under the Law, it doesn't matter what we give.' Of course, it is seldom argued from the point of view that a tithe is too little to give! But there are other issues too. There are so many needs. How do we decide where to give? Churches, charities, needs at home and abroad all desperately require financial support and are frequently asking for help. I find my own reactions vary from compassion to despair, gratitude, guilt and frankly sometimes even cynicism. To ensure we are giving what God wants us to give and in the right places we need to look at four aspects of giving.

1 Attitude

> Giving is not about an amount. God does not look at what we give, He looks at what we keep for ourselves. God looks at our hearts. It is all about attitude.

God values our action on the basis of our attitudes. God's attitude to giving is clear. John 3.16 tells us, 'For God so loved the world that He gave his one and only Son' (NIV). Because God loved He gave. He sets the perfect example of giving motivated by love. An attitude of love in giving is essential. 'If I give all I possess to the poor ... but have not love, I gain nothing' (1 Corinthians 13.3 NIV). It is hard to think of anything much more commendable than giving everything to the poor, but if it is done with the wrong attitude and without love it will bring no benefit whatsoever to the giver. In God's economy the attitude is far more important than the amount. Jesus stressed this in Matthew 23.23:

84

'Woe to you, teachers of the law and Pharisees, you hypocrites! You give a tenth of your spices – mint, dill and cumin. But you have neglected the more important matters of the law – justice, mercy and faithfulness. You should have practised the latter, without neglecting the former.' (NIV)

Even though the Pharisees had been meticulous in their giving Jesus rebuked them. He looks past the amount of the gift to the heart of the giver.

> For giving to be of any value it must be done from a heart of love.

If we are giving to a church or merely to meet a need this is only charity. But if we are giving to the Lord, our Creator, Provider and Saviour in love and gratitude, it is an act of worship.

> True giving is an expression of love and gratitude to God.

We are also told that we should give cheerfully. 2 Corinthians 9.7 says, 'Each man should give what he has decided in his heart to give, not reluctantly or under compulsion, for God loves a cheerful giver' (NIV). The original Greek word for cheerful is *hilaros*, 'hilarious' – we are to be hilarious givers. So how do we develop this habit of hilarious giving? In 2 Corinthians 8.1–3 Paul writes about the church in Macedonia:

And now, brothers, we want you to know about the grace that God has given the Macedonian churches. Out of the most severe trial, their overflowing joy and their extreme poverty welled up in rich generosity. For I testify that they gave as much as they were able, and even beyond their ability. (NIV)

How did they manage to give so generously in spite of their extreme poverty? The answer is found a little later in verse 5: '. . . they gave themselves first to the Lord, and then to us in keeping with God's will' (NIV). From this passage it is clear that the key to cheerful giving is to submit to Christ and to ask Him to direct us as to how much He wants us to give. Only then are we in a position to receive the advantages that God wants to give.

> 'The principal hindrance to the advancement of the Kingdom of God is greed. It is the chief obstacle to heaven-sent revival. It seems that when the back of greed is broken the human spirit soars into regions of unselfishness.' (O. S. Hawkins, American pastor and author)

Our offering should therefore express our faith in God, our commitment to Christ and our concern for the advancement of His work in the world. It should not be a duty but a joy, an act of celebration as we honour the source of all our blessings and wealth – God our Heavenly Father.

Generosity is a wonderful attribute but we can only practise it when relationships are more important to us than possessions. Giving generously is about enriching ourselves as we are being generous in giving to others. Nothing is a clearer barometer of our commitment to Jesus, our gratitude to Him and our concern for others in need than our readiness to be financially generous. A person who is committed with their cheque book is committed indeed. Furthermore, Christians who are generous will motivate others to be generous too. Many believers today have not been taught about giving or, if they have received teaching, they have not been responsive to it. They need to see other Christians using their money and possessions enthusiastically to help further God's Kingdom. If they see really joyful giving they will respond with the same enthusiasm. When Christians are generous and have the right motives God has promised to enable them to be continually generous to others.

2 Advantages

> It is in giving that we receive and in letting go that our lives can be enriched.

Obviously a gift should benefit the recipient, be it church, charity or individual, but incredibly, in God's economy, if a gift is given with the right attitude, the giver benefits even more than the receiver. Acts 20.35 tells us that Jesus said 'It is more blessed to give than to receive' (NIV). It is clear that the giver benefits in the following areas:

Increase in closeness

Above all else giving directs our attention to Jesus. Matthew 6.21 tells us, 'For where your treasure is, there your heart will be also' (NIV). As we give our gift to Him and it is distributed according to His will we will certainly be drawn closer to Jesus. We will experience the exciting feeling of having money to give in particular ways that make us feel as if we are directly co-operating with God in His mission. Remember too that giving is one of the responsibilities of a steward and the more faithful we are in the discharge of these duties the more we can 'enter the joy of the Master'. Nothing in life can remotely compare with entering in His joy and knowing Christ more intimately.

Increase in character

God wants us to trust Him for the future. He does not want us to be unrealistic but neither does He want us to be so hesitant that we do not trust Him to provide for us. He wants us every day to be more conformed to the image of Jesus. The character of Christ is that of an unselfish giver. We humans are selfish by nature and giving sacrificially is a major way in which we can be more like Jesus who gave everything for us.

> Giving is not God's way of raising money. It is God's way of raising people in the likeness of His Son.

Increase in heaven

Too often we find ourselves distracted by houses, cars and retirement plans. The moment we die all these concerns are going to be irrelevant. Matthew 6.20 tells us to 'store up for yourselves treasures in heaven, where moth and rust do not destroy, and where thieves do not break in and steal' (NIV). Imagine staring into eternity with nothing to show for our time here on earth. The length of our life and the things we substitute for God's will would suddenly appear insignificant. But we can invest in eternity by bringing people into the Kingdom.

As a young Christian I was involved in running a youth group. One thing that this group of young teenagers did was to mark a basic Bible study course which was done primarily by people in the Third World. Each month several of the students would ask for a Bible and the young people clubbed together to buy Bibles to send to all those who requested them. On one occasion they received a request from a person who was being held in a high security prison and they dutifully sent off the Bible. About two months later we received a reply which affected us all very deeply. The letter said this:

> I cannot begin to tell you how joyous I felt when the Bible came. I have been reading it for hour after hour and it has been a great strength to me. I have also been sharing its teaching here in the prison and I am delighted to tell you that six prisoners here have become Brothers in Christ as a result. I am not sending the next part of the course back. We are all being executed tomorrow.

The kids from that youth group are going to get some welcome in heaven – and what is more they are going to have for ever to rejoice. They probably went without magazines and sweets to be able to buy those Bibles – but oh, what a reward!

Increase on earth

> Don't give to get – God isn't a slot machine. But give expectantly.

Prosperity teaching – if you give to God He will multiply things tenfold and so you will become rich – is a travesty of biblical truth. But God will give material blessings to a generous giver. 'One man gives freely, yet gains even more ... A generous man will prosper; he who refreshes others will himself be refreshed' (Proverbs 11.24–5 NIV). Also in 2 Corinthians 9.6–11 we see that giving results in a material increase:

> Whoever sows sparingly will also reap sparingly, and whoever sows generously will also reap generously. Each man should give what he has decided in his heart to give, not reluctantly or under compulsion, for God loves a cheerful giver. And God is able to make all grace abound to you, so that in all things at all times, having all that you need, you will abound in every good work. As it is written: 'He has scattered abroad his gifts to the poor; his righteousness endures for ever.' Now he who supplies seed to the sower and bread for food will also supply and increase your store of seed and will enlarge the harvest of your righteousness. You will be made rich in every way so that you can be generous on every occasion, and through us your generosity will result in thanksgiving to God. (NIV)

It is essential to see why God will give you more. It is so that you can be 'generous on every occasion'. So when you give do so with a sense of expectancy.

> To hear from God, give to somebody and then realize that you are an answer to prayer, is terribly exciting.

3 Amount

> 'A man there was, tho' some did count him mad,
> The more he cast away, the more he had.'
> *The Pilgrim's Progress*, John Bunyan, 1628–1688)

Paul defines the reason for having wealth as being able to meet the needs of the other saints. The gift of giving is defined as the foundation for life of selfless devotion to others. Being a wealthy Christian brings greater responsibility. Whether we are rich or poor is a matter for God – He will only give us what we are capable of handling. But the duties and responsibilities of wealth are heavy because of the temptations. It is easy to adjust lifestyle to include lavishness and indulgence, curtailing giving at the same time. Our responsibility is sobering. Most of us in this country are rich by worldly standards and God has, in His eternal plan, decided to use us to supply the resources for His work. One day we will all have to stand before Him and give an account of how we have handled His resources. For any true believer that must be a real motivation!

When you give, never qualify your giving by comparing it with what others give. To do so will make it seem either insignificant or all important. It will never be either. So how much should we give?

> A £50 note and a 50p coin started talking in a bank. 'I go to nice shops, good restaurants and health clubs,' the £50 note said. 'How about you?' The 50p coin replied, 'I go to church a lot.'

The tithe

Tithing, or giving one–tenth of your income, is mentioned throughout the Bible. It is often said that the tithe is Old Testament legalism. But Abram tithed in Genesis 14 after returning from the daring rescue of Lot. He met Melchizedek the priest and *voluntarily* surrendered to him one-tenth of all that he had. This took place 430 years before the Law was given to Moses.

Although the tithe was mentioned in the Law, no punishment was indicated for not tithing and therefore tithing has always been a voluntary act for God's people. But although not compulsory, tithing with proper motives brings blessings from God.

'Bring the whole tithe into the storehouse, that there may be food in my house. Test me in this,' says the Lord Almighty, 'and see if I will not throw open the floodgates of heaven and pour out so much blessing that you will not have room enough for it.' (Malachi 3.10 NIV)

Ideally, the local church should serve as the 'storehouse' today. After all, God intends the Church to carry out certain functions which include looking after the poor and needy and reaching out to the lost at home and abroad. But even if your church is not doing all these things and you would like to support a Christian organization that is, remember you cannot sit under the teaching of a local church and not support it financially.

Jesus commends tithing in the New Testament in Matthew 23.23. Whilst He condemned the manner in which the Pharisees tithed, He indicated that this was what they should have been doing.

Is the tithe the limit?

The tithe was never meant to be the limit. In fact, if Christians gave the same amount to the Church as the Jews used to give, nearly one quarter of their income, there would never be unmet economic needs in the ministry. We would be able to support church workers as never before, have debt-free buildings and be able to meet all kinds of needs head on. God uses 10 per cent as a starting point. We are not compelled to give more but grace is not a licence to do nothing. After all, God doesn't just own the first 10 per cent – He owns the lot, which is why we should never tithe with the view that the remainder is ours. Like tithing, any giving beyond it should be an outward expression of willingness and obedience to put others first. Others may be called by the Holy Spirit to give more. Yet others may have the gift of giving as mentioned in Romans 12.8. People with this gift tend to be very prudent, living disciplined lives and being especially sensitive to the needs of others.

So where does this leave us today? My firm beliefs are as follows:

- Everyone who is working should tithe. However, if you have substantial debts, and have made every possible sacrifice yourself first, you should set aside at least 10 per cent of your income to clear the debts and then use that money for giving after you are out of debt.
- Those who are on benefits, and thus have not earned any income, should give what they can. That is why the story of the 'widow's mite' is so powerful. Remember that God looks at what we hold back, not the amount we give.
- Many of us need to be giving far more than 10 per cent. Jesus gave everything for each one of us. Sometimes we can put something in the collection plate and five minutes later forget that we've even given it. For our giving to be true giving it needs to be sacrificial.

4 Approach

Jesus tells us to give in such a way that our lifestyle is affected. 1 Corinthians 16.2 clearly shows us how we should approach our giving. 'On the first day of each week each one of you should set aside a sum of money in keeping with his income' (NIV). We can see from this that our giving should be:

- periodic – on the first day of every week
- personal – each one of you
- a priority – on the *first* day
- premeditated – set aside money in keeping with income
- private – what we give should always be to honour God and not ourselves

Therefore as a rule the only people who know how much you give should be you, your partner and the recipient. Matthew 6.1–4 says:

'Be careful not to do your "acts of righteousness" before men, to be seen by them. If you do, you will have no reward from your Father in heaven. So when you give to the needy, do not announce it with trumpets, as the hypocrites do in the synagogues and on the streets, to be honoured by men. I tell you the truth, they have received their reward in full. But when you give to the needy, do not let your left hand know what your right hand is doing, so that your giving may be in secret. Then your Father, who sees what is done in secret, will reward you.' (NIV)

Areas of giving

We are told to give in a variety of areas. To whom and in what proportion is something that each one of us has to pray through. Frequently I have people tell me there is no point in giving because the needs are so enormous they can never be met. When I hear this I invariably recount this story:

> A man was walking along a seashore after a storm. During the storm many shellfish had been washed onto the shore and as he walked the man was picking some of them up and throwing them back into the sea. Another man joined him. 'Why are you throwing those shellfish back into the sea?' he asked. 'There are millions here. It makes no difference.' The first man quietly replied, 'But it makes a great deal of difference to the ones I throw back.'

I believe that when we pray earnestly about our giving, God will tell us which 'shellfish' are ours. In other words, he will lay on our hearts countries, needs, individuals, charities that he wants us to support. God doesn't want emotional givers, he wants obedient ones.

Seeking God's wisdom before giving

There are a wide variety of questions that we need to ask as good stewards before we decide to give and these include:

- Who are the people/organization asking for the money? If

you are not personally familiar with the organization ensure you get sufficient literature and information to enable you to make an accurate assessment.

- Is the true message of Jesus Christ being communicated?
- Is there a positive response and are lives being changed as a result of their ministry?
- Are the lives of those in leadership positions consistent with biblical principles? Never give to ministries whose leaders have lavish lifestyles.
- For what purpose will funds be used? If necessary ask for a budget and accounts.
- How much money is spent on fund–raising and how much on actually doing the job?
- Is the organization achieving its goals?
- Is the work expanding? Ask around and be discerning. Pay a visit to meet the relevant people if that is appropriate.
- Does the organization have a reputation for excellence both inside and outside of church circles?
- Can you find out what other Christian organizations say about them?

Church, Christian workers and charities

Throughout the Bible there is a focus on the maintenance of God's ministry. 'I give to the Levites [priests] all the tithes in Israel as their inheritance in return for the work they do while serving at the Tent of Meeting' (Numbers 18.21 NIV). The encouragement to give in this way continues in the New Testament. 'The elders who direct the affairs of the church well are worthy of double honour, especially those whose work is preaching and teaching' (1 Timothy 5.17 NIV). God never intended that his servants should have to struggle to survive, but because of the disobedience and selfishness of others it happens all too often. Hardly a week goes by without at least one minister ringing the Credit Action helpline for help. In one case a church, of a major denomination, had allowed its financial affairs to get into such a mess that the local bank account had been frozen. No one would tell the denomination headquarters so nothing was done and eventually the minister had a nervous breakdown and had to stand down. Not only is this an appalling human tragedy but as a witness to the outside world it is indefensible.

Family

We are called to support our family, be it elderly parents or our own children. Increasingly in our society we see these principles being flouted, with some parents being abandoned as they are 'too expensive to keep' and in other cases parents dying and leaving their children not a modest inheritance but significant debts. This is not biblical. 'If anyone does not provide for his relatives, and especially for his immediate family, he has denied the faith and is worse than an unbeliever' (1 Timothy 5.8 NIV).

The poor

Jesus identifies with the poor and needy. Matthew 24.40 tells us that whatever we do for those suffering on earth we are actually doing it as if to Jesus. And if that truth is staggering then the reverse is terrifying – *when we do not give to the poor we leave Jesus hungry and thirsty.*

During Jesus' earthly ministry He consistently gave to the poor and this was also confirmed by the early disciples. When Paul announced his ministry to the Gentiles, 'All they asked was that we should continue to remember the poor, the very thing I was eager to do' (Galatians 2.10 NIV).

If we are not giving to the poor it can affect us in the following ways:

Prayer
'If a man shuts his ears to the cry of the poor, he too will cry out and not be answered' (Proverbs 21.13 NIV).

Provision
'He who gives to the poor will lack nothing, but he who closes his eyes to them receives many curses' (Proverbs 28.27 NIV).

Intimacy with God

Failing to share with the poor will prevent us from entering into
an intimate relationship with God. '"He defended the cause of the
poor and needy and so all went well. Is that not what it means
to know me?" declares the Lord' (Jeremiah 22.16 NIV).

Wouldn't it be good to try and follow the acts of Job: 'I rescued
the poor who cried for help and the fatherless who had none to
assist him . . . I made the widow's heart sing . . . I was eyes to
the blind and feet to the lame. I was a father to the needy; I took
up the case of the stranger' (Job 29.12–16 NIV).

A plea to Christian leaders

Please do not be afraid to talk about giving! If you teach God's
people the joys and responsibilities of giving you will be helping
set free people from their bondage to money. The aim is not to
raise money, but to increase their trust, dependence and joy in
our loving God. Remember too that we should be looking to fellow Christians for financial support and not the non-believers
we are attempting to reach with the gospel. Can I also invite you
to ask yourselves where your giving is going? It is easy to keep
spending money in certain areas because that's where it has
always gone. But can I ask you to dig deeper? For example, is
too much time, money and energy being bound up in maintaining a building at the expense of other things? After all, Jesus
commanded His disciples to go out and convey His good news
to people in the world.

Christian or secular charities?

My own belief is that it is right to direct virtually all giving to
Christian work – there are plenty of non-Christians who will give
to secular charities but will not give to Christian ones. However,
as always, do listen to God's prompting in this.

Giving through our work and time

We should also be adopting a giving attitude towards our work and our 'spare time'. 'Whatever you do, work at it with all your heart, as working for the Lord, not for men' (Colossians 3.23 NIV). If you have little available money but plenty of free time, ask the Lord to show you where He wants you to give that time.

Impact of giving

It is important to remember the impact of your giving. £15 will feed a child in the Third World for a month or provide the funds to carry out a simple cataract operation enabling a blind person to see. In this country it would mean that six families who are in debt could receive a self-help guide free of charge or it could support a mentally handicapped resident in a Christian home. It could also provide Bibles and other Christian literature to win people into the Kingdom.

Giving can have a major impact on both giver and receiver. Several years ago I lost my job in the City and received a redundancy cheque. From this I set aside a sum of money that I felt God was telling me to have ready to give. Two years later it was still intact and I must admit I was beginning to wonder about my communication channels! Then one day at a Christian conference I met a minister from one of the poorest countries in the world. Over dinner we were talking and I asked him what was the biggest problem he faced. He said that in the area where he lived the desert had been encroaching on the arable land, and to add to their problems they had not had any rain for four years. I asked whether anything could be done, and he told me that if they could plant trees in a certain area it would stop the sand funnelling down. I asked him how much it would cost to plant the trees. It was exactly the sum God had told me to put aside two years earlier. I must admit that my first reaction was 'Oh no, Lord, not all of it!', but I repented and as my heart began to pound I told him what had happened and that the money was available. He was so excited he rushed off to telephone home.

When he eventually came back he was grinning from ear to ear. 'We are so grateful to God,' he said, 'but my friend back home also told me something that will really bless you. It started raining in my town half an hour ago.' I was elated. My first thought was, Oh Lord, give me an overdraft, as I wanted to give all that I had! I felt as if I was walking on air for weeks afterwards.

The point of this story is this. God would have brought the rains in any case. But if I had not been faithful in giving I would never have known that they came. It was like a heavenly confirmation. God really does generously bless a faithful giver.

Giving goals

'I'm afraid biblical charity is more than merely giving away that which we can afford to do without.' (C. S. Lewis, 1898–1963, English scholar and apologist)

It is important that giving goals are set. I believe God will quite clearly give you and your partner areas in which He wants you to give.

Think about and discuss with your partner all the various needs there are in the Church today. How do you choose? What priorities has God given you? How well informed are you? Could you do more? When you have thought and prayed about where God wants you to give, it is a good idea to complete a 'giving plan'. As the sums mount up you can see your dreams being realized and this is a real encouragement and blessing and will probably make you want to try and do even more. Look at the example shown in Table 10, given to help you see how it works. Once Fred and Freda had paid for the child's holiday they maintained their giving and, in their case, rather than start giving to a new source they increased their commitment to the two other charities they were already supporting.

Make sure that when you come to do this you make your giving as tax-effective as possible by using covenants or Gift Aid. Organizations such as Sovereign Giving or the United Kingdom Evangelism Trust will be able to help you maximize your giving.

Table 10 **Giving plan** (example)

Fred and Freda

				Receivers of giving		
Date	Amount	Balance	St Martin's	Missionary Society	Help the Poor	Child's First Holiday Charity
1.1.96	200	200	100	20	30	50
1.2.96	200	400	200	40	60	100
1.3.96	200	600	300	60	90	150
6.3.96	(−150)	−150				Child's holiday
		450				fully sponsored
1.4.96	200	650	400	100	150	
1.5.96	200	850	500	140	210	

Organizing your estate

On average it will take less than two hours' planning to arrange distribution of what could well have been over 40 years or more of accumulation – yet seven out of ten people do not make a will. To die without a will has several drawbacks:

- The law will eventually decide who receives your assets. This will depend on, for example, the number of close relatives you have. Any priorities that you may have had or beneficiaries you had in mind will not be taken into account.
- Heirs may well be faced with significant legal fees for working out the estate.
- The estate could well be subject to higher taxes than would have been the case with wise tax planning.
- The guardians chosen to raise your children may not have been the ones you would have chosen had you made a will.

Anyone who knows Jesus as Saviour and Lord has a solemn duty to provide for his family and this includes planning for your loved ones should you die before them. People usually avoid making a will for four reasons:

1 a reluctance to face death
2 procrastination
3 a belief that they have too little to make it worth while
4 the cost of drawing up a will

Old or young, married or single, rich or poor, you should still draw up a will and complete the 'organizing your estate' sheet. Isaiah said to Hezekiah, 'Set your house in order; for you shall die' (2 Kings 20.1 NASB). One day, unless Jesus returns in the meantime, we will all die. One of the greatest gifts we can leave our families at such an emotional and stressful time is an organized estate. Please do not leave it any longer. You never know the plans God has for you.

Once you have completed the sheet, review it carefully with your partner and older children. After reviewing it, give a copy to your bank or solicitor and any friend or relative who may be involved in helping to settle your estate.

Have a look at Fred Smith's version (see Table 11) before completing your own.

Table 11 **Organizing your estate**

Date 1.1. 96

WILL

The Will is located: *Best Bank, Mytown*
The person desgnated to carry out its provisions is: My wife Jane
If that person cannot or will not serve the alternative is: Henry Cooper
Solicitor: I. M. Rich   (phone) 0179 123567
Accountant: Count Numbers (phone) 0123 234678

INCOME BENEFITS
1. Company Benefits:

On my death, if on company business, my company will pay to my heirs a sum equivalent to three times my annual gross salary. If not on company business, one year's gross salary. You are not entitled to ongoing company pension.

2. Social Security Benefits:

The office you should go to is located at *100 High Street Mytown*. This should be done promptly as delay could mean loss of benefit. Take with you:

- my death certificate
- your birth certificate
- our marriage certificate
- birth certificates of each of the children

3. Life Insurance

a) Insurance Company: English Widowers   Policy Number: NB12345
   Value: £80,000
   Person Insured: Fred Smith   Beneficiary: Jane Smith

b) Insurance Company: Rock Solid Insurance   Policy Number: CD13579
   Value: £80,000
   Person Insured: Jane Smith   Beneficiary: Fred Smith

FAMILY INFORMATION

Family member name	Address	NI Number
Fred Smith	1 Hill View, Mytown	CD123789
Jane Smith	1 Hill View, Mytown	NW246890
Jill Bloggs	3 The Lakeside, Goole	PW3355669
Jack Smith	1 Hill View, Mytown	QR2244660

FUNERAL INSTRUCTIONS

Undertaker: *The Co-op, 50 High Street, Mytown.* Tel: 123456
To be buried at: *St John's, Mytown.*

I confirm that the following memorial gifts be given to:
St John's Church, Mytown   £200
Housing the Homeless   £500

Conclusion

'For I will not offer burnt offerings to the Lord my God which cost me nothing.' (2 Samuel 24.24 NASB)

If every committed Christian in this country tithed giving would increase nearly ninefold. It is obvious from that figure that we will struggle even to maintain our current level of witness, never mind show any signs of growing outreach. When Christians do not plan their giving they usually have nothing to give. All of us tend to allow our standard of living to drift upwards in line with our income. Regardless of the work to which we are called, nearly all Christians can give something, and when that is done in love it exemplifies the greatest sacrifice ever made for humankind – the death of Jesus on the cross. Jesus gave out of love when He left heaven to come to earth. It was love that enabled Him to give His life so that we could be saved from our sins. And God the Father was also motivated by love when He gave His only Son for you and me.

How we use our money demonstrates the reality of our love for God. In many ways it can prove our love more conclusively than Bible knowledge, length of prayers or position within the Church. All of these can be unreal, but the way each one of us uses his or her money and possessions shows clearly what we really believe.

Ask yourself

Martin Luther said, 'Every man needs two conversions, one of the heart and one of the wallet.'

1 What do I think of this statement?
2 Have I had my second conversion yet?
3 What is God saying to me about my attitude towards giving, my level of giving and my priorities?
4 What prevents me from sharing my possessions?
5 In what practical ways could I share my possessions more freely?

6　Do I give solely to honour God?
7　Do I periodically evaluate the where, when and how of my giving?
8　Do I have a genuine concern for others – especially the poor, needy and lost?
9　Do I store up all my treasures in heaven?
10　Ask your partner: Do you think we give too much/too little?

5 SAVING

This is the third chapter running where the title could make many Christians feel guilty. I have come to the conclusion that Christians feel guilty when they haven't got much money and they feel guilty when they have plenty! 'Shouldn't I rely on God alone to meet my needs and trust Him alone to provide for the future?' 'If I save aren't I depriving God of the opportunity to meet my needs?'

I am often asked such questions by people who have a real desire to live in complete faith, trust and dependence on God. To answer such questions I believe it is vital to distinguish between faith and presumption. The Bible clearly shows that 'walking in the light' means putting total faith and trust in God alone. However, it also shows we have a personal responsibility to display wisdom, make sensible decisions and choices and also demonstrate sound personal discipline. Saving is therefore our responsibility, to manage wisely the blessings that God has provided. Failure to save anything at all from our income is presuming on God and demonstrates foolishness rather than faith. Proverbs 21.20 tells us that only a fool saves nothing.

Verses that seem to legislate against saving

The following verses seem to legislate against any form of saving:

'Do not lay up for yourselves treasures upon earth where moth and rust destroy, and where thieves break in and steal.' (Matthew 6.19–21 NASB)

Jesus said, 'If you wish to be complete go, and sell your possessions and give to the poor, and you shall have treasure in heaven.' (Matthew 19.21 NASB)

He summoned the twelve and began to send them out in pairs. And he instructed them that they should take nothing for their

journey except a mere staff; no bread, no bag, no money in
their belt. (Mark 6.8 NASB)

On the surface these verses appear to indicate that no one should
save, but they are, in fact, not general principles but advice for a
specific circumstance or to combat greed. In fact, Jesus also uses
examples of how saving should be carried out – but it needs to
be done for the right reasons and in keeping with God's will. In
the parable of the talents we see this clearly, as the man left his
servants and entrusted his property to them, an exact parallel of
what Jesus has done to us. Both the servants with five and two
talents invested the money well and doubled it and this pleased
the master. 'Well done, good and faithful servant. You have been
faithful with a few things. I will put you in charge of many things.
Come and share your master's happiness' (Matthew 25.21 and 23
NIV). But to the servant who was given just the one talent and
failed to do anything with it he said, 'You wicked, lazy servant!
. . . You should have put my money on deposit with the bankers,
so that when I returned I would have received it back with interest' (Matthew 25.26–7 NIV).

The most important thing to remember here is that it is wrong
to invest just for the sake of making money. The reason for
investing is to hear the Lord saying to you, 'Well done, good and
faithful servant'. Making money should be a by-product of doing
what God has called you to do. Also remember that peace of
mind does not come through accumulation of material possessions. If it did the wealthiest people in the world would also be
the happiest. Instead they often feel depressed and miserable.
True peace only comes from God. If we put Him first then we
can invest and save for His purposes, once we have already given
generously.

It is not money itself but the wrong attitude towards it – the
love of money – that is the root of all kinds of evil. In the Old
Testament many of the godliest people (for example Job, Abraham and David) were extremely wealthy. Other godly people
lived in abject poverty. But whether we have much or little, to
allow what we have to dwindle away through poor management
is bad stewardship. However, simply to multiply and store money

without purpose is hoarding. Jesus explains this clearly in the parable of the rich man and his barns.

> 'The ground of a certain rich man [note he was already rich] produced a good crop. He thought to himself, "What shall I do? I have no place to store my crops." Then he said, "This is what I'll do. I will tear down my barns and build bigger ones and there I will store *all* my grain and my goods. And I'll say to myself, "You have plenty of good things laid up for many years. Take life easy; eat, drink and be merry." But God said to him, "You fool! This very night your life will be demanded from you. Then who will get what you have prepared for yourself?" This is how it will be with anyone who stores up things for himself but is not rich towards God.' (Luke 12.16–21 NIV)

Although I feel I could write a book about this parable alone, there are two key points here. First, despite already being rich the man was trying to find a way to store *all* his goods. *All* is the key word here. It is only biblical to save when we are also giving generously because 'where your treasure is, there your heart is also'. If we concentrate only on our savings then our priorities will move in that direction – we will be drawn to possessions. But if we balance our savings by giving generously then we will still have Christ at the centre of our finances. The second point here is that this applies to each one of us. Look again at Luke 12.21. 'This is how it will be with *anyone* who stores up things for himself.' I must admit to sometimes wishing this verse said 'This is how it will be for *some* of you' and then I could exclude myself! Luke 14.33 says 'Any of you who does not give up everything he has cannot be my disciple' (NIV). So before we can begin to even think of saving each one of us has to give up everything!

As we learn to invest money according to God's principles we will find that He will increase our opportunities to help other people. This is, in reality, the real purpose of investing – to increase our assets so that we can serve God more fully. We are all going to be accountable to God for everything we do, including how we manage His money.

Acceptable reasons for saving

There are several acceptable reasons for saving and these include:

To provide for your family

'If anyone does not provide for his relatives, and especially his immediate family, he has denied the faith and is worse than an unbeliever' (1 Timothy 5.8 NIV). This basically means you should provide for your old age so that you and your immediate family are not a burden on others. See pp. 135–7.

To leave an inheritance

It is certainly right to leave some money for your children but ensure it is never enough to spoil them or make them think they will never have to work because you will be providing for them. Proverbs 13.22 tells us, 'A good man leaves an inheritance for his children's children' (NIV).

To help children at particular times

This may be, for example, to help a child through college or to pay for their wedding.

> . . . children are not responsible to save up for their parents, but parents for their children. (2 Corinthians 12.14 NASB)

> I have seen a grievous evil under the sun; . . . wealth lost through some misfortune, so that when he has a son there is nothing left for him. (Ecclesiastes 5.13–14 NIV).

Certain sums need to be set aside regularly over a long period to meet special future needs. Every effort should be made not to use this resource for anything other than what it was intended for.

To enable you to become involved in full-time ministry

One objective would be to enable you to save enough to give up some or all secular employment so that you can devote more time to working for God if this is the plan He has for you.

Unacceptable reasons for saving

We do have to be honest about our savings and ask when enough is enough. We should not be hoarding for some vague pretext or the fear of some unlikely future event. The desire to be rich is strictly forbidden. 1 Timothy 6.9 says, 'People who want to get rich fall into temptation and a trap and into many foolish and harmful desires that plunge men into ruin and destruction' (NIV). This is not *some* people, it is *all* people. *Everyone* who wants to get rich will fall into this trap. The next verse shows another reason why we should not want to get rich. 'For the love of money is a root of all kinds of evil. Some people eager for money have wandered from the faith and pierced themselves with many griefs' (NIV). Matthew 6.24 tells us we cannot serve both God and money. So when we want to get rich we are actually loving money and therefore hating God. This does *not* mean being rich is wrong. There is nothing wrong with being wealthy if our wealth is the by-product of being a good steward.

So how do we overcome the temptation to get rich? Paul advised Timothy to 'flee from all this [the desire to get rich] and pursue righteousness, godliness, faith, love, endurance and gentleness' (1 Timothy 6.11 NIV). If you believe there is even a chance you have such a desire determine to replace it with godliness. Try to work out what is causing the desire and then set about overcoming the temptation. For example, if you have a habit of buying too many fashionable clothes, then don't visit shopping centres even if you say you are only going to 'window shop'. The chances are that is not how it will end up! Also submit to God. We can do this with every confidence because Jesus overcame a massive temptation to become rich and powerful. After he had fasted for days in the wilderness the devil tempted him three times and the final temptation was this:

The devil led him up to a high place and showed him in an instant all the kingdoms of the world. And he said to him, 'I will give you all their authority and splendour, for it has been given to me and I can give it to anyone I want to. So if you worship me, it will all be yours.' (Luke 4.5–7 NIV)

Jesus could have owned every material possession but he was able to resist the temptation because he was totally submitted to God the Father. I believe, therefore, that our Heavenly Father will never ultimately prosper us if we are motivated by a desire to be rich. Loving money equates to greed and according to Colossians 5.5 greed is idolatry.

Starting to save

Most people do not save regularly. In fact the average person in this country has no savings. Regular fixed obligations to support a relatively high lifestyle, significant monthly credit commitments and a total dependence on next month's salary to keep within these limits means there is no surplus to save. But the Bible encourages us to do so. Proverbs 21.20 says, 'In the house of the wise are stores of choice food and oil, but a foolish man devours all he has' (NIV). Whilst debt puts pressure upon the future, savings make provision for tomorrow, and this requires self-denial. Given the fluid state of the jobs market and the fact that there are rarely 'jobs for life' any more, this is particularly important.

How and how much to save

The most effective way to save is regularly to allocate a sum of money to your savings account after you have set aside what you are giving to God. A regular deduction from your pay can help here. There are two types of saving and these are long term and short term. Long-term savings are intended to fund requirements such as retirement income. Once saved they should not be used for any other purpose – indeed in some cases there may be severe tax penalties for doing so. Short-term savings are designed to help you plan future spending – such as replacing your car.

Short-term savings should also be set aside to cover emergencies such as illness or loss of income. An ideal emergency fund would be equivalent to six months' income.

If you are to become a successful saver you must consistently spend less than you earn and save the difference over a long period of time. Savings grow as the result of compound interest just as debt grows when the interest is working in reverse. There are three features of compound interest: the amount saved, the interest rate earned and the length of time you have been saving. The key element is time. Assuming a 10 per cent return on £1,000 per annum invested between the ages of 21 and 28 (i.e. £8,000 saved) it will be worth over £425,000 at the age of 65. However, if you waited until you were 29 and then saved £1,000 a year until your 65th birthday (i.e. £37,000 saved) it would be worth less than £365,000, so start saving today!

Ten steps to establishing clear-cut savings goals

1 Know where the Lord wants you to invest

It is vital that all savings decisions are covered by much prayer. It is God who should direct us. If we ever feel uneasy about investing in a certain area or wonder if what we are doing might be unethical then we should not do it. 'I am the Lord your God who teaches you to profit, who leads you in the way you should go' (Isaiah 48.17 NASB).

2 Decide on the categories of saving

No one should invest without having an ultimate purpose for the money. To do this you first have to know your financial condition so that you can provide for your needs and accomplish your objectives.

'For which one of you, when he wants to build a tower, does not first sit down and calculate the cost, to see if he has enough to complete it? Otherwise, when he has laid a foundation and is not able to finish, all who observe it begin to ridicule him.' (Luke 14.28–9 NASB)

Let us look at some realistic goals:

Retirement
There is nothing wrong with retirement planning provided it is kept in balance. Many people look forward to retirement only because they hate their present job. Of course, a Christian never retires from active service for God and we should always be where we feel we can serve God best. To be in that position we may sometimes need to lay money aside to supplement an expected reduction in income later on. In fact retirement savings can allow you to volunteer to work for a Christian organization without the need for a salary. Early and regular investments in a pension scheme also help here. The long-range goal of retirement will vary depending on the age, income and pension provisions of each individual. I will be looking at retirement in more detail in the chapter on work.

Preservation
Imagine you had inherited £20,000 and you felt it essential that this money was preserved until your retirement as you really will need it then. A couple starting out with nothing must first develop a surplus and look for investments that will help it grow, but someone who has inherited £20,000 should look first to the preservation of that money. You are not so much concerned with the return *on* your money as you are with the return *of* your money, i.e. you cannot afford to take risks which could mean you might lose some or all of it. An investment of a one-off windfall will be very conservative. The goals would be not to maximize the growth but to minimize the losses and achieve a reasonable return.

Education
Unlike those who are trying to preserve a windfall, a family with their children's education in mind must think more in terms of

growth, again depending on the amount available to invest and the length of time it can be invested.

Income
A couple approaching retirement will be looking for maximum income to live on whilst they will also be concerned about the preservation of their assets.

Growth
Everyone would like to see their investments grow. A growth strategy means that there is little immediate need for the funds but a sizeable future one.

Tax effectiveness
It is also important that every advantage is taken of lawful ways of maximizing returns. It is bad stewardship for non-taxpayers to have any capital invested where income is taxed at source. Other government-approved investments allow interest to be paid gross if money is kept for a certain period of time – so long-term savers should take full advantage of such situations.

3 Evaluate risk and return

An important factor in investing is called the risk/reward radio. The guideline on this is: the higher the rate of return the higher the degree of risk. Education and analysis can lower risks but they cannot totally eliminate them. Before investing in anything, look at the potential risks and then ask if you can afford to take them. Investing in a major bank, building society or company will be the safest investment but will also have the lowest returns.

The answers to questions about risk normally depend on age and purpose. The older you are the less risk you can afford to take, because it is more difficult to replace the money. But if the purpose of the money is for, say, retirement which is still many years away then you can probably afford to take a slightly higher risk. But beware – look at the Living Bible translation of

Ecclesiastes 5.13–15: 'Savings are put into risky investments that turn sour and soon there is nothing left to pass on to one's son. The man who speculates is soon back where he began – with nothing.'

It is vital to avoid 'get-rich-quick' schemes. Be very wary if any of the following are offered to you:

- The prospect of a high return or profit that is 'virtually guaranteed'. You cannot get something for nothing.
- Something that requires an immediate decision. This is often put across as a 'favour' that is being granted to you which you will miss out on unless you decide straight away.
- Any risk being minimized, ignored or dismissed.

Remember before making an investment consider your decision prayerfully and patiently and in consultation with your partner to ensure that it is within God's will for you. Most 'get-rich-quick' schemes attract people who don't know what they are doing, encourage people to risk money they cannot afford to lose and attract people who will make instantaneous and emotional decisions. Exactly what some American 'prosperity' teachers do when you come to think about it!

4 Be patient

'Steady plodding brings prosperity' (Proverbs 21.5 LB). A wise investor will always keep some cash on hand for emergencies but in reality, given the ease of access on bank and building society accounts, this does not have to be very large. It is important to get your money working for you and patience will help avoid a great many errors. Remember most investments look good initially. Know what your goals and objectives are and only select the investments that are going to help meet them. Usually greed and speed go hand in hand, so a key to avoiding greed is patience. 'He who makes haste to be rich will not go unpunished' (Proverbs 28.20 NASB).

5 Diversify

There are no absolute guaranteed investments on earth. You only have to look at events in the City of London in recent years to know that even major, respectable institutions can crumble overnight. Therefore we need to ensure that we 'don't put all our eggs in one basket'. We need to diversify to minimize the risks. 'Give portions to seven, yes to eight, for you do not know what disaster may come upon the land' (Ecclesiastes 11.2 NIV). It is important to remember that the principle of diversification is not a one-off decision. You have to keep on managing your money. We need to be good stewards of God's property. If you feel ignorant, seek advice but also try and gain your own knowledge. Having worked in the City for twenty years I think I can say that if you studied the various forms of investing for one hour every day for six months you would know a lot more than most people who are selling them!

6 Follow long-term trends

Always invest with an eye to long-range economic trends and particularly keep a watchful eye on inflation levels. In a non-inflationary economy you can invest in banks and building societies and generally keep even. But in an inflationary economy you can miss out and so will need to have money invested in index-linked savings where the interest paid is dependent on the level of inflation. 'Any enterprise is built by wise planning, becomes strong through common sense and profits wonderfully by keeping abreast of the facts' (Proverbs 24.3–4 LB). Inflation is an evil for all but especially for savers. It helps foster an attitude that the future is always worth less than the present and this creates a world view totally at odds with biblical truth. Years of inflation can thus increase the 'spend now' message but as inflation also eats away at the ability of governments to fund benefits fully it is vital to invest during these periods.

7 Seek advice about timing

Seek godly advice as to the timing of your investment. 'There is an appointed time for everything. And there is a time for every event under heaven' (Ecclesiastes 3.1 NASB). The right investment at the wrong time is in fact the wrong investment.

8 Know where to sell

Before you buy always know where you can sell your investment – particularly if it is something collectable such as stamps or coins. Never trust the salesman who says, 'If you ever want to sell we'll buy it back.' Invariably when you go back he no longer works there and no one else knows what you are talking about. Remember too to shop around. For example, there have recently been so many cases of endowment policies being surrendered that people have set up in business buying and selling them and can often, particularly on an older policy, get better prices than the surrender value you would be offered by your insurance company.

9 Train the members of your family

All partners and children old enough to understand should be trained in the principles of sound saving. In Britain in about 80 per cent of cases a wife will outlive her husband. So a wife needs to know about money management and savings strategy. She needs to know how to buy and sell and where to go for help when she needs it. Also, because sometimes both parents may die together in an accident, older children should be brought into these family decisions. At least leave written instructions on the best way of managing these assets whilst at the same time minimizing the pressures of Inheritance Tax.

10 Count the cost

Every investment has a cost which is not just financial. There are time commitments, the effort required and sometimes emotional stress. So look at all aspects of the investment, not just the cash return.

Biblical instruction to successful investors

Financial bondage can also exist through having too much money. The accumulation of wealth and material pleasures of life can be an obsession that can destroy one's health, fragment family unity, promote separation from friends and block God's will. Everything and everybody can become objects to be used on the ladder of success. The trouble is we usually define a rich person as someone who has more money than we do! But given the standard of living in this country, many of us, in world-wide terms, are rich and we therefore need to take heed of the warnings given in the Bible and apply them in our lives.

Do not be proud

'Thus said the Lord, ". . . Let not the rich man boast of his riches; but let him who boasts boast of this, that he understands and knows me"' (Jeremiah 9.23–4 NASB). Wealth naturally tends to promote pride but, as I have said, God does not value us according to our status, job, income or assets. He looks at our hearts. 'Instruct those who are rich in this present world not to be conceited' (1 Timothy 6.17 NASB).

Do not trust riches

As we become successful at saving it is so easy to start putting our trust in our own provision for ourselves. But at all times we need to keep Jesus central to our thinking and put all our trust in Him. 'Do not fix . . . hope on the uncertainty of riches, but on God who richly supplies us with all things to enjoy' (1 Timothy 6.17 NASB).

Give generously

'Command them to do good, be rich in good deeds and be generous and willing to share. In this way they will lay up treasures for themselves as a firm foundation for the coming age, so that they may take hold of the life that is truly life' (1 Timothy 6.18–19 NIV).

Do not become inaccessible

'Woe to those who add house to house and join field to field, until there is no more room, so that you have to live alone in the midst of the land' (Isaiah 5.8 NASB).

Pay a fair price

There may be times, particularly if you become an expert in certain types of saving, that you spot a bargain. If this is because the seller is ignorant of the real value as a Christian you must point that out to him. 'You shall not wrong one another' (Leviticus 25.17 NASB).

Lend generously

Once you start accumulating savings and becoming relatively wealthy your responsibilities increase. You may well be asked to lend more to the poor, especially within your own church. If you are asked please seriously consider doing so at no interest and in no great expectation of it ever being repaid. 'Give to him who asks of you, and do not turn away from him who wants to borrow from you' (Matthew 5.42 NASB). You will be blessed in your generosity. 'It is well with the man who is gracious and lends' (Psalm 112.5 NASB).

Insurance

Trusting God doesn't mean that we shouldn't have any insurance policies. Though we trust Him totally we still have a duty to manage our affairs in such a way that our dependants are protected and our legal obligations fulfilled. Therefore future family needs should be protected with life assurance. A good steward will also insure against financial disaster by having house and contents insurance. Of course, all of us are legally required to have proper car insurance.

The whole purpose of insurance is to reduce or eliminate the risk of loss. There are many types and these include: car, accident, redundancy, sickness, life and disability. The amount and type of insurance you need will differ from person to person but will follow the guidelines of the previous paragraph. Some may find it impossible to afford all the insurance they need to protect their family. Others may well be overinsured with every conceivable possibility being covered. In either case it is important to do two things. First pray about the level and types of insurance that God wants you to have. Second, because it can be complex and difficult to understand, seek experienced advice before making any decision. Remember to balance the advice of the insurance salesman by talking to at least one other person you trust who has nothing to gain from your insurance purchase.

Savings goals

Sometimes it is a great encouragement to keep track of your progress in savings and watch them grow. Once you have reached your goal in saving for an item then you may buy it without going into debt. The Savings Goals sheet (see Table 12) is designed to show you how to record the date, description and amount of each deposit or withdrawal from savings. You are then able to allocate the saving over a number of items and calculate the balance of your total savings as well as of each item.

How to use the savings form

Think about and discuss with your partner what you feel you could and should save for. Are there any items you could save up and pay cash for that you previously would have purchased using credit? Once you have done this, estimate the amount you will need to save for each item. Then determine which of these are priorities. Look at the example of Peter and Mary White (Table 12). This couple have established four savings goals:

- £3000 for their daughter's wedding
- £600 for furniture
- £5,000 for a replacement car
- long-term savings for retirement

Table 12 **Savings goals** (example)

Peter and Mary White

| TOTAL SAVINGS | | | | Item | | | |
Date	Description	Amount	Balance	Wedding	Furniture	Car	Retirement
	Estimated cost			£3,000	£600	£5,000	Undetermined
	Monthly Amount			£ 50	£ 50	£ 50	£ 50
	Beginning balance		5,000	500	500	1,000	3,000
				25	25	25	25
1.1.96	Jan savings	100	5,100	525	525	1,025	3,025
				25	25	25	25
16.1.96	Jan savings	100	5,200	550	550	1,050	3,050
				25	25	25	25
1.2.96	Feb savings	100	5,300	575	575	1,075	3,075
				25	25	25	25
16.2.96	Feb savings	100	5,400	600	600	1,100	3,100
20.2.96	Bought furniture	600	4,800		−600		
					Nil		
				25		50	25
2.3.96	Mar savings	100	4,900	625	50	1,150	3,125
				25		50	25
16.3.96	Mar savings	100	5,000	650	50	1,200	3,150

1 Take the amount of your existing savings and allocate it into the beginning balances total. (Peter and Mary have £5,000 saved. They have allocated £500 for the wedding, £500 for furniture, £1,000 for the car and £3,000 for retirement.)

2 Allocate the monthly amount you intend to save for each item. (Peter and Mary plan to save £200 a month and have allocated £50 for each of the four categories.)

3 When adding to savings, write in the date and allocate the sum according to the items for which you are saving.

4 Add this to the running balances.

5 When a purchase is made, subtract this from the savings balance.

6 Once you have purchased an item, allocate the amount you were saving to another item. This sum may be added to an item for which you are already saving or you may wish to add a new item. (In Peter and Mary's case, once they had saved enough to buy the furniture they added the £50 towards the car.)

Ask yourself

1 Am I able to save a little each month?

2 Am I providing for my family's future?

3 Do I balance my saving with generous giving?

4 Does my saving demonstrate good biblical stewardship?

5 Do I have specific rather than general savings goals?

Think about your insurance needs. Remember individual circumstances will often dictate very different answers to these questions.

6 Is my and my partner's life cover adequate?

7 Do I need to insure against unemployment or sickness?

8 Do I think Christians never need to take out insurance because we can trust God for everything or do I think we should take out insurance to cover every eventuality as we are called not to be a burden on family or society?

9 Ask your partner: Do you think we are saving too much/too little?

One guaranteed investment

As I conclude this chapter I feel I should add that there is one guaranteed investment. It is an unswerving faith in God and recognition that He sent His only Son to earth to take all our sin and die on our behalf so that we can live for ever. This investment is a free gift which is available to all who call upon the Lord Jesus Christ. If you do not know the freedom and peace of mind that only Jesus can bring talk to someone at your local church or even give me a call at Credit Action.

6 MANAGING MONEY IN THE FAMILY

Most of this chapter will be involved with handling money sensibly and biblically and teaching children to do the same. But before we look at that in detail it is vital that you and your partner are totally open and in agreement about all money matters. Sadly, I say this because I am often approached by one partner with money worries and in the *majority* of cases they have not told their partner the whole truth about their current financial situation. This is a recipe for disaster. You may not want to worry your partner but, as I have said before, if you fail to admit to the truth there will be a breakdown in trust which could do far more damage to your marriage than any debt problems you might face. It is so important that you look at money together, decide on your priorities in budgeting, giving and saving and then work to fulfil them. That is why at the end of many of the chapters in this book I have asked you to ask your partner how they perceive your ability to handle money in various key areas. Please don't lose your temper because of what your partner tells you, but do reflect and pray about it. Sometimes the truth hurts!

Teaching our children

Think back to when you first left home. How well prepared were you to make good financial decisions? We may well have learnt all sorts of things from our parents and teachers but usually we are taught very little about how to handle money. I believe we need to teach our children in three ways:

1 Spoken teaching

'These commandments that I give you today are to be upon your hearts. Impress them on your children. Talk about them when you sit at home and when you walk along the road, when you lie down and when you get up' (Deuteronomy 6.6–7 NIV).

2 Teaching by example

Our children need a role model. Paul recognized the importance of this in 1 Corinthians 11.1: 'Follow my example, as I follow the example of Christ' (NIV). God has given us the perfect example in Jesus and we should model our lives on Him. It is very important that our walk matches our talk.

3 Practical teaching

Learning to handle money is a vital part of every child's education. Parents should encourage their children in the following areas:

Income

It is my opinion that as soon as a child starts junior school he or she should be given a small sum of pocket money to manage. Parents need to decide whether some or all of the income should be earned or whether it is simply an allowance. The amount of income will vary according to the financial circumstances of the family, the child's age and his or her ability to earn. The amount is not important but the responsibility is. At first it will be a new experience and you should expect your child to make quite a few mistakes. Do try and let things take their natural course. If all of your child's income is spent on the first day on an unwise purchase and there is therefore nothing left for the rest of the week do *not* come to the rescue – these mistakes will prove to be the best teacher in the long run. As parents you should try and establish boundaries and offer advice on how to spend the money but at the end of the day your child must have the responsibility of freedom of choice. It is only by doing so that they can start to learn how to prioritize their spending.

Budgeting

As soon as children start to receive an income teach them how to budget. You could even begin with three small boxes labelled 'give', 'save', 'spend'. Even a very young child can understand this method because when the box is empty there is nothing left to spend!

I believe that by the time children are going to secondary school they are old enough to be involved in the family budget. They will appreciate that they are being regarded as 'growing up' because they are now being involved in the plans for spending the family income. As they mature they should participate in every aspect of the family budget. This will help teach the limits of the family income and how money has to be stretched in so many different directions to meet all the family needs.

At first your child may think that the family has so much income it would be almost impossible to spend it all but when the cost of housing, motoring and food are fully appreciated you may experience a rapid softening of position! During the early teenage years ask your children to show their budget explaining how last week's money was spent. Only then give the next week's allowance. It is at this time too that you need to teach your children to be sensible consumers. They need to learn shopping skills, to appreciate the difference between needs and wants and to learn to trust God financially. The dangers of advertising and impulse spending also need to be spelt out.

Debt

It is vital to teach children about the cost of money and how easy it is to get into debt and how hard it is to get out of it. They need to know that compound interest works both ways and that interest of only 5 per cent may be paid to you if you are in credit but you may be expected to pay 20 per cent or more if you are in debt.

Giving

This should be established as soon as possible as a major priority. It is a good idea, especially for young children, for the giving to be directed at a tangible need. For example, if they buy tinned food which is then distributed to the poor and needy they will see the direct impact their giving is having. With older children it is a good idea to involve them in the decision-making process as to where to give. The more they can be involved with their parents and the more their views are listened to and respected the better habits they will have developed by the time they are adults.

Saving

The habit of saving needs to be established at an early age. As the child grows you can explain the benefits of compound interest. Once this is fully understood your child is likely to remain an habitual saver and thus know financial stability as an adult. Children can be encouraged to save short term for things like a toy, but also long term – perhaps for a car on their 17th birthday. Some parents have found that their children are motivated to save if they also agree to make a contribution to long-term savings but I'll leave that decision to you!

Money-making

Parents also have the responsibility to train children in the value of work. If your child responds well and learns how to work with the proper attitude then they will not only have learnt about contentment but will also have made themselves much more employable. Areas of training needed here are:

Learning routine responsibilities

You do not become managing director overnight! The best way for a child to become a faithful steward at work is to establish the habit of doing daily jobs around the house. These are responsibilities given to each child that should be carried out well for the benefit of the whole family.

Your attitude to work

Many children today do not have a real grasp of what their

parents actually do to generate income. If you can expose them to your work that is excellent, but if not, take time to explain your job to them. I was very humbled recently when someone asked my wife what I did for a living. 'He helps people manage their money responsibly,' Carole replied. Then my four-year-old John said, 'Yes, but he also teaches people about Jesus and that's more important.' Out of the mouth of babes!

Because most children do not see their parents at work, our attitude and habits around the house are a major modelling influence. If I work hard at the office but then complain about doing the washing-up at home what is being communicated to my children?

Earning extra money

You should encourage your children to do extra work to gain extra money. If your child has to find extra money for something like a school trip encourage him or her to earn the money to pay for it by doing extra work around the house.

Encouraging your children to work for others

Doing a paper round, waiting at tables or baby-sitting are all part of education. This type of part-time job gives your children their first opportunities to enter an employer/employee relationship. The object of training your children in the value of work is to build and discipline character. A hard-working child with a good attitude will be a more rounded and satisfied person. They will grow up with more respect for the value of money and the effort required to earn it.

Gifts

In addition to allowances and payment for jobs you may period-ically want to give your children a spontaneous gift. A gift is unasked for, unearned and often undeserved. It is given out of unconditional love.

General points

First of all may I simply say that if your children are to learn from you you have to spend time with them. Buying things for them simply will not do – they need to be a major priority in your life. As my good friend Rob Parsons of Care for the Family says, 'Who on his death bed wishes he had spent more time at the office?' Sadly, I know from looking at my own life that it seems easy to find time for work but then be too exhausted to spend time with my children.

Another valuable lesson we can teach our children is to encourage them to experience God's provision through prayer. God can and will answer our prayers supernaturally and something provided by Him is going to be so special.

Remember as well the impact of television – it has been calculated that a child born today will on average watch television 25 hours a week and will have seen one million adverts by the time he or she is 25 years old. By and large television reflects society's values – not God's – so it does not have to be overtly anti-Christian material that can adversely affect our children. We need to remember this.

As parents we are always walking a tightrope with regard to money. We need to keep a proper balance. A few are too miserly, but in our affluent society far more are too indulgent. Overindulgence with money is damaging. It slows the development of a child's character and destroys both motivation and initiative. Far too often it creates in a child a regular expectation that they will be given things without having done anything for them in return.

A strategy for independence

Finally, you need to establish a strategy of independence for your children. Remember to communicate verbally the biblical principles of handling money. You could even give them this book to read! Be models of financial faithfulness so that they can see how you apply these principles and create practical opportunities for your children to experience God's principles. Children will differ significantly in character and temperament, so tailor the training to fit your child, but also be both persistent and consistent. By doing this you will leave your children with the wonderful legacy of financial faithfulness.

Helping your children become financially responsible

One of the most important things we can do as parents is to ensure that when our children leave home they are well equipped to deal with financial matters. I have produced a checklist (see Table 13) to help you see how they are progressing. This should be reviewed at least once a year. Look at the example to help you.

Table 13 **Children's review** (example)

Income

Are your children receiving an income?
Yes.
Are they performing routine jobs around the house in return for that income?
Yes.
What must they purchase with their income?
Magazines, sweets, games.

Budgeting

Are the children budgeting?
Yes.
Describe how they are doing this.
They are using a basic exercise book with columns for spending, saving and giving.
Are your children involved in family budget discussions?
Michael participates but Kate is too young.

Saving

Do your children have a savings account?
Yes.
Do they appreciate the concept of compound interest?
Michael does.
How much do they understand about savings?
So far only that the bank pays them interest on their account.

Debt
Have you taught your children the biblical principles of debt?
Michael.
Are they aware of the true cost of credit?
Yes.

Giving
Have you taught the principles of giving?
Yes.
Describe their giving.
Michael gives 50p to church and Kate 20p.

Routine responsibilities
What unpaid jobs around the house do the children do?
Clean their rooms and take out the rubbish.
How do you hold them accountable?
We check their rooms weekly.

Your work
Do your children understand the need to earn a living?
Yes.
How would they describe your job?
Daddy builds houses. Mummy builds a home.
Could they help you at work in any way?
They are not yet old enough.

Extra money
Can your children earn extra money about the house?
Yes.
How?
Cutting the grass – Michael.
Washing up – Kate.

Working for others
Do your children do jobs for others?
Michael cuts next door's grass.

Strategy for independence
**What strategy are you using to ensure your children will be
financially sound when they leave home?**
We are slowly increasing their responsibilities for money management
and expect them to be responsible for all their needs, except food and
shelter, by their last year at school.

Ask yourself

1 Do I communicate openly and honestly with my partner about money?
2 Do I keep my promises to my children as dependably as to an adult?
3 Do I think children should get pocket money for doing nothing?
4 Do I think if they did more around the house I would give them more?
5 Am I happy with my family's financial goals?
6 In what practical ways can I show my children the importance of giving?
7 In what ways am I passing on any materialistic world views to my children?

Ask your partner:

8 Do you think I handle money responsibly?
9 How could I better handle my money?
10 Do I accept financial responsibility well?

7 WORK

Work is not only a means of creating wealth but also a way of distributing it. Not only that but it also has other aspects that have a direct impact upon people. It brings routine, purpose, identity, friendships and an ability to be in control of your own situation. Therefore its loss can cause all sorts of problems including fear, anxiety, depression, loss of self-worth and ill-health. These are problems which are affecting more and more of us and yet they are not readily being addressed. The long-term security of a 'job for life' is rapidly disappearing. Part-time work and short-term contracts increasingly rule the day. And as world-wide competition increases and multi-national companies shop around for the cheapest work-forces these trends can only continue. As loss of employment has been the major cause of debt in this country in recent years it is easy to see how important these trends are for all of us.

A biblical perspective

God instituted work *before* the fall. 'The Lord God took the man and put him into the Garden of Eden to work it and take care of it' (Genesis 2.15 NIV). Thus God sees work as necessary. Paul says in 2 Thessalonians 3.10, 'If anyone will not work, neither let him eat' (NASB). Now this does *not* apply to those who are unable to work either through illness or because there are no jobs available. It applies to those who could work but deliberately choose not to. When we work we should remember that God has given each of us specific skills – we are all different and no one is superior to anyone else. Also we should always remember that any success we achieve is in fact down to God and so we should thank Him for any promotion and not 'blow our own trumpet'.

When we work we are actually serving the Lord. 'Whatever you do, do your work heartily, as for the Lord rather than for men . . . It is the Lord Christ whom you serve' (Colossians 3.23–4 NASB). This means we need to work hard: 'Whatever your hand finds to do, verily, do it with all your might' (Ecclesiastes 9.10 NASB). Our work should be of such a high standard that people never equate mediocrity with God. We must always do the best we can. It is tragic that some of us try to share the gospel with our co-workers whilst at the same time being shoddy and irresponsible in our work habits. The way we work often says so much more about us and our level of faith than our words. But remember to keep work in balance – too much time spent there can mean neglect of your Lord and your family. All Christian employees should be:

- honest – there should never be any reason for condemnation. Bear in mind that as a Christian you will be watched very carefully so this applies to time-keeping and diligence as well as the use of the office phone or photocopier.
- faithful – it is vital that we always work obediently to the best of our ability.
- prayerful – remember to pray about your well-being at work and especially bring to the Lord any problems you are facing there.

Always strive to:

- honour your employer – work hard and try not to gossip about his failings – have you ever looked in a mirror?
- honour your fellow employees – help your colleagues by working hard and encouraging your co-workers. Try and avoid office politics.
- be open about your faith – If you are working as well as you can you have every right to let others know of your faith. Share with them what brings you peace of mind and contentment.

Work and ambition

The Bible does not condemn ambition outright – but it does if it is selfish.

But if you harbour . . . selfish ambition in your hearts, do not boast about it or deny the truth. Such 'wisdom' does not come down from heaven but is earthly, unspiritual, of the devil. For where you have envy and selfish ambition, there you find disorder and every evil practice. (James 3.14–16 NIV)

The motivation for our ambition should be to please Jesus. In our work we should strive to please Him by doing everything to the best of our ability.

Work and calling

Every one of us has a specific calling which God intends us to fulfil in our work. 'For we are his workmanship, created in Christ Jesus for good works which God prepared beforehand, that we should walk in them' (Ephesians 2.10 NASB). God has given us the appropriate skills, ability and desire to accomplish this work. For many this call will be to remain in secular work. God wants His children in the factory and the office as well as in the church.

Redundancy

During the recession in the early 1990s about 25 per cent of the workforce experienced redundancy. I believe the levels of employment in this country are likely to remain volatile and therefore redundancy or loss of hours is something we must be prepared for. If it does happen to you these are some of the things you should bear in mind, as it will invariably alter your financial situation.

Look at your situation at work

First of all, if you have a contract, examine it. Employers have to consider such things as length of service, experience, behaviour and attendance records. If you feel you have been treated unfairly or singled out let them know and even consider complaining to the Advisory Conciliation and Arbitration Service (ACAS). If you are near retirement age you may be offered early retirement instead of redundancy. This can be a good option if you think you will struggle to get another job as you may be able to draw your pension benefits early.

Check your redundancy pay

Make sure you are getting at least the minimum requirements. If in doubt seek advice from your Union or your local Citizens' Advice Bureau.

Check your tax

Redundancy payments are tax-free up to £30,000. Anything above that is taxed normally so if this applies to you it could be worth putting some of the excess into pension provision.

Check your benefit entitlements

If you have been working since leaving school or college you may have little knowledge of how the benefits system works. It is important to 'sign on' as soon as you finish work, not just to get your unemployment benefit but also to ensure that your National Insurance contributions are paid.

Ensure you are budgeting

Refer back to the chapter on budgeting, but particularly consider the following if you have just been made redundant:

1 Contact all real and potential creditors explaining what has happened.
2 Talk to your mortgage lender to see if they can help you in any way.
3 Remember if you have limited assets you should eventually get help with your housing payments either through Housing Benefit if you are renting or Income Support for mortgage interest. Remember you may well have taken out

a mortgage protection policy and if so don't forget to apply quickly.

Use your money sensibly

If you have been given a lump sum of redundancy money do not invest it all at 5 per cent interest if you have debts where you are being charged 25 per cent interest. Clear the most expensive debts first. Do not tie up any money long term until you are sure you will not need it in the near future.

Check your insurance and pensions

It is always worth asking your employer whether they will extend your insurance cover and pension plan for a few months whilst you try and find another job.

Look for another job

Take time and produce a good CV, join a Job Club, use your contacts and read the newspapers.

Acknowledge your emotions

Losing your job can bring shock, fear, depression and loneliness. But remember you have probably lost your job through no fault of your own. Don't ask, 'Why has this happened to me?' Ask instead, 'What do you plan for me now, Lord?' God doesn't see you as a failure because you no longer have a job – and so neither should you. Wait and watch for His perfect plan to unfold.

Retirement

The dictionary defines 'retirement' as a 'withdrawal from active life'. This goal of retirement is deeply ingrained in our society with many, many people actively looking forward to it and imagining that they will be blissfully happy doing nothing but pursuing a life of leisure. However, there is no biblical basis for retirement as long as one is physically and mentally capable of working. The concept of 'putting someone out to grass' is not biblical. Age is no obstacle to God. He will provide the necessary energy you need to fulfil the work He has ordained for you. For example, Moses was 80 years old when he began his 40 years of leading the Children of Israel in the desert. It may well be that God changes the nature of work – to make it less physically demanding and more reliant on experience and wisdom – but a Christian never retires from active service. We have a major problem when we begin to say that once a person reaches a certain age he or she is no longer productive and must therefore be replaced by a more assertive, younger person. This cannot be supported historically or biblically. Look at the example of Paul. He chose to continue his missionary journeys giving no thought to retirement as long as he was able to carry out the work that God had given him to do. He was still actively travelling in his late sixties.

As I mentioned briefly in the chapter on savings, in itself planning for retirement is not wrong. Proverbs 6.6–8 tells us, 'Go to the ant, you sluggard; consider its ways and be wise! It has no commander, no overseer or ruler, yet it stores its provisions in summer and gathers its food at harvest' (NIV). When we are at our most productive, probably between the ages of 30 and 60, it is sensible to store some of the surplus to ensure that when our ability to earn declines we are not a burden on our children. However, as Christians, we must ensure we do not store up too much. Many of us have developed a mania about retirement and the supposed need for storing large amounts of assets. Often we will already have over-provided but will continue to build up further reserves. Money that could be used to help bring the gospel to the lost or food to starving children is sitting in a retirement account because it enables us to claim tax relief on it. This is hoarding. It is unlikely that you will spend as much in retirement as you did when you were working and bringing up a family. In fact, your living costs should decline significantly.

Think about who you would rather trust to provide for your retirement – you or God. Begin to try and work out how much you really will need for expenses such as food, clothes and holidays. If you find you have overcommitted your income to retirement planning perhaps you could now give some more to God's work. You cannot suffer if you possess the right attitude.

So to conclude, there is nothing wrong with saving and planning for your retirement but there is everything wrong with unnecessarily storing up cash believing that this is the *only* way to provide for your later years. God is more than capable of supplying your needs in your old age.

Ask yourself

1 Do I work hard so as to be a good example to those in my work place?
2 Do I work hard to enable myself give generously to God?
3 How is my time-keeping?
4 Am I always totally honest in the way I handle my company's equipment, phone, stationery, etc.?

8 THE ETHICAL USE OF MONEY

> 'We must recover reverence for the earth and its resources, treating it no longer as a reservoir of potential wealth to be exploited but as a storehouse of divine bounty on which we utterly depend.' (William Temple, 1881–1944, Archbishop of Canterbury)

Ethical investment and banking cover a wide range of concerns which include:

- social factors – levels of pay, working conditions, health and safety
- company standing – the honesty and integrity of companies, the quality of their management, the good stewardship of human and material resources
- environmental factors – lack of pollution, nuclear waste and animal testing, the recycling of waste products, the lowering of energy consumption, etc.

Producers, investors *and consumers* can influence any event involving the use of money. In particular consumers can choose one product rather than others purely on ethical grounds and the reason for doing this is at least as valid as any economic one and certainly far more important than any of the non-rational reasons advertisers ram down our throats. Investors too can send an important message to producers and manufacturers if they start to boycott certain goods because they believe they have been produced unethically.

Christians should therefore both buy and invest to the best of their knowledge in an ethical way. Doing so brings pressure to bear on companies to come into line with ethical principles. To some degree this has to be done by showing disapproval of bad practices, but the major emphasis should be on encouraging good practices, sound working conditions and responsible environmental stewardship.

Stewardship of the earth's resources

As I have mentioned throughout this book, a steward is someone who has been asked to look after someone else's property and at some stage the steward will have to give an account as to how he or she has managed that property. The issue of stewardship has become of great concern today in regard to the exploitation of the earth's resources. In the past we have naively believed that we could continue to extract fossil fuels and chemicals from the earth and alter the whole nature of countries by draining rivers and deforestation. In addition, we have nonchalantly emptied our waste products, which include nuclear and toxic material, into our seas without any real concern for the consequences. Furthermore the whole world's economic system is based on the premise of continued and sustained growth, but already there are signs that we are rapidly reaching nature's limit. If this continues I believe it is possible that next century's wars could be fought over forests and drinking water.

It is vital, therefore, that we exercise careful stewardship of our world's finite resources. If we continue as we are, competition for resources can only increase and this will mean that stronger economic countries will be better able to compete for these resources. As such the rich countries will be exploiting the poor as they desperately strive to maintain growth and quality of life for their inhabitants.

It is this neglect of stewardship of the earth that has already produced much of today's poverty. Behind our Western economic assumptions of continued expansion is complete unreality. Have a look at Table 14, which lists the differences between North and South, to see how extreme the situation is already. These figures indicate to me that we Christians have to have a wider definition of Christian stewardship. It is not simply about raising money for the Church; it is also about understanding that God made the whole earth for us all to enjoy and that we should use the resources wisely. We should never be greedy and never exploit those who are too weak to defend themselves. Sadly, when we look at the figures in Table 14 we can see that that is exactly what is happening at the moment.

Table 14   **Our world today**

North	South
25% population	75% population
80% income	20% income
Life expectancy 70+ years	Life expectancy 50 years
Nearly all have enough food	20% don't have enough food
Uses 88% of natural resources produced	Uses 12%
Eats 70% of grain	Eats 30%
Eats 80% of protein	Eats 20%

[Source: Christian Aid]

Every minute 30 children under the age of five are dying of malnutrition.

So why do we live in such a divided world when in theory there is enough food for everyone? The answer in a nutshell is greed. The answer is self. It begins with me. In this country, and especially in the Third World, people go hungry not because there is a shortage of food but because they cannot get to it. Every society determines who is entitled to what. This will usually depend on whether a person owns land, works, earns money and has dependants. Therefore, it simply comes down to power.

As Christians we need to go back to the creation account and remember that the earth and its resources are a gift from God and we are called to ensure that these resources are available to all humankind. These principles are built into Old Testament teaching – particularly the Year of Debt Release and the Year of Jubilee (found in Leviticus) – but seem absent from Christian thinking today. In Jesus' time some corn would be left in the farmers' fields so that the poor could come along and gather it (even on the Sabbath!).

Just as we need rest, so the land needs fallow years when it can be restored, but in the rush for growth, the mix of overpopulation by the poor and over-consumption by the rich it has made it more and more difficult to start eliminating poverty. Furthermore the fair distribution of food and other essentials has not been able to keep pace with the increase in population.

> The cry of the poor is for justice, not charity.

Attempts to improve the lot of the Third World have so far been costly failures, mainly because they have been worked out on Western terms. For example, back in the 1970s many Western banks lent extensively to Third World countries. This was fine until interest rates rose sharply and the countries were unable to service the loans, particularly as the value of most of the products these countries were exporting fell at the same time. Loans could not be repaid and the International Monetary Fund made many countries cut back public spending sharply which meant loss of jobs. This combined with other measures hit the poorest hardest.

I believe that environmental issues raise questions that all Christians in the West must face. Can we legitimately pursue our own wealth regardless of the harm it may be doing others? Are we bold enough to contrast our living standards with the needs of the poor rather than looking enviously at our neighbour's lifestyle? We must remember that any time our beliefs cut across the sinful selfish practices of others, particularly if it threatens their lifestyle, we are likely to be opposed. If we put God first there will be criticism and retaliation every time we confront the materialistic nature of our greedy society. Some may even lose their jobs for opposing unfair or dishonest policies, but we have to make a stand. So what can we do?

Follow good examples

We have the examples set by well-known leaders such as Mother Teresa as well as other fellow-believers. Their example should inspire us to use material possessions in such a way as to help people in the Third World rather than exploit them.

Live more simply

All of us should be aiming to live a simple lifestyle. This should not be induced by guilt but as we alter the way we live and we realize the impact that the release of our resources is having elsewhere, I believe it is something we will *want* to do more and more.

Use your power

So many of us feel there is nothing we can do, but in fact we can do plenty. It takes relatively few letters to an MP before he begins to question his position on an issue. Look at the pressures applied when Shell Oil wanted to dump an old oil rig in the Atlantic Ocean. Consumer power led to a complete reversal of policy. Would France, for example, have gone ahead with its recent series of nuclear tests if everybody who opposed them had boycotted French products? Let's stand up for what we believe in.

Look at how and where you invest your money

This is an important question for all Christians. Where do you bank? Do you know how they use your money? Where is it invested? At the time of writing the only major bank in Britain with a policy of ethical investment is the Co-operative Bank. That is why Credit Action has chosen to bank there. If we have savings, pensions or insurance we should also be ensuring that these are invested ethically as well. Put simply, ethical investment allows individuals to invest in a socially responsible manner without compromising their principles or beliefs. The first such fund, the Friends Provident Stewardship Fund, was launched in 1984. Its aim was to achieve long-term growth through investment in companies that had a proven commitment to social responsibility, whilst avoiding those that could be environmentally damaging or those that exploited people or animals. Thus investments follow one of two routes:

1 Those that contribute positively to the environment:
   - environmental protection
   - pollution control
   - conservation/recycling
   - safety
   - medicine
   - *All these would be included.*
2 Those which have a negative impact on the environment:
   - armaments
   - animal experimentation
   - alcohol
   - tobacco
   - pornography
   - gambling
   - any environmentally damaging practice
   - *These would not be included.*

The combination of the success of the Stewardship Fund, together with increasing public awareness of these issues, has meant that there are now around 20 such companies. The more people who invest in this way the more pressure is imposed on companies to review their strategy and become more socially responsible. If you need advice on ethical investment you should contact a firm of Christian financial consultants, such as Ethical Financial, who would be able to offer independent advice and answer any questions you may have.

Watch what you buy

See 'Practical ways of using your money ethically' at the end of this chapter. Many products that we buy without thinking about – chocolate bars, for example – start with raw materials that are produced and purchased in the Third World. Are we aware what producers are being paid for their cocoa, coffee beans, sugar cane, etc.? Are they being paid a fair price or is someone along the line being exploited? Often, unless you buy shares in a company and go along to its annual general meeting and ask some awkward questions, you will find it hard to find out. Alternatively, as coffee, tea and sugar are major exports of several Third World countries, buying these products on a fairly traded basis is an excellent way to have a beneficial impact on these countries' economies. Persuading local supermarkets to stock such brands is also very helpful and usually not too difficult. Britain's first ethical supermarket has already opened in Bristol. Called 'Out of This World', it will not sell goods that are tested on animals, considered damaging to the environment or contain artificial additives. A chain of 200 such stores around the country is planned. In the energy-saving stores meat and vegetables will be organic, washing powder will be bio-degradable, and slimming and tobacco products will be banned.

There are other promising moves in this area. First, our good friends at the Jubilee Centre are pursuing a policy of encouraging 'relational' audits in many areas of our society ranging from prisons to companies. As the name suggests, the aim here is to encourage co-operation and ensure that there is no exploitation of any group. It is likely that any company which is prepared to have a relational audit is already making strenuous efforts to ensure that no such exploitation occurs.

Second, other organizations are beginning to produce 'social' audits. These look at the social, economic and ethical effects of its business in the areas in which it operates. Traidcraft plc, a Christian company, not only produce financial accounts each year but they also produce social accounts. To give guidelines as to the impact of social audits below is an extract from Traidcraft's social audit so you can see just what they are trying to achieve:

> Traidcraft's primary business objective is to increase the volume, value and quality of fair trade with primary producers in the 'third world'. Their goal is to increase the transfer of wealth from the 'first world' to economically disadvantaged people in the 'third world' by creating opportunities for small farmers and craft producers to sell their products in the cash rich 'first world'. Traidcraft sees this strategy as an alternative to long-term aid which will increase producers' capacity to determine

their own future. They also seek to demonstrate that trade with the 'third world' on fair terms is commercially viable.

Traidcraft do not set up their own suppliers. Rather they work with suppliers that:

- are locally owned and managed
- are organized primarily for the benefit of the producers
- pay fair wages
- provide better-than-average working conditions
- encourage the producers' involvement in ownership and decision-making

As well as this they make a commitment to:

- pay fair prices
- make advance payments where needed
- not switch to other suppliers just to get lower prices
- develop long-term business relationships
- act and campaign on behalf of producers to eliminate barriers to Third World trade
- inform customers about the producers and their products

In addition they monitor the environmental impact of their actions in the following areas:

- energy consumption
- disposal of toxic substances
- waste-paper recycling
- packaging consumption
- product development

Their purchasing policy states that:

Production methods should take account of the need to protect the natural environment. The products and production methods used should be appropriate to the economy and ecology of the country of origin. Locally available raw materials and technology should be used wherever possible. With food products, trading which encourages competition for land between essential subsistence farming and exports, and trading in staple crops where people's diets are deficient should be avoided.

The way Traidcraft operates has a message for each one of us. The company's dominant culture springs from the Christian ethics of love and justice. It is not just historically Christian, it continues to reflect the essential nature of Christian living.

Keep up to date with what is happening in the world

In this way if you hear of exploitation or abuse you can steer clear of the products and companies involved.

Develop an interest in a particular Third World country

By doing so you can quickly become an expert and help influence Christians on a local or even national scale should needs or abuses occur. You could consider giving up one two-week holiday, and instead use your skills working in a Third World country. Your own life might well be changed! To find out more, ask about the Short-term Service Directory at the Christian Service Centre.

Start on your own doorstep

What can you do to help meet the needs in your immediate locality? Are you really aware what they are?

Change the way you live

Try and waste as little as possible and recycle as much as you can to restrict your use of the earth's limited resources. For example, if you are using recycled paper you are saving trees. This preserves the forests and thus prevents dust bowls. Dust bowls cause soil erosion, which stops crops growing, and this is a major cause of famine.

By taking small but consistent steps in our daily lives we can make a positive contribution towards the world becoming less hungry.

Practical ways of using your money ethically

Use public transport where possible

As I have said, a major feature of why we should try and use our money ethically is because non-renewable resources are being used up. Government policies, such as pushing up taxes on petrol, can affect our use of these resources, but in the end it is our personal decision as to whether we choose to cut back our consumption or not. It is undeniably more healthy for both ourselves and the environment if we decide to walk or cycle more on short journeys and use public transport on longer ones. If we need a car we should try and have one which uses unleaded petrol or if it is an older model at least get a catalytic converter fitted.

Recycle waste

We also need to consider carefully what we do with our waste. My 4-year-old has already been taught about recycling at school and more of us parents need to be practising this. Aluminium cans, bottles and paper can now easily be recycled. Buying recycled paper products and using only scrap paper for phone messages and shopping lists, etc. can also contribute to this process. Many clothes, rags, newspapers and oils that we throw away can again be recycled. Recycling centres are becoming easier to find, but if there isn't one near you contact your local council.

Reduce fuel consumption

One of the main causes of energy loss in a typical building is poor insulation. This accounts for an astronomical fuel bill which is far larger than necessary. Roof insulation, draught excluders and double glazing can help heat loss here. We need to switch off lights and any other electrical gadgets when they are not in use. The subsequent reduction of energy consumption of fossil fuels would help prevent both global warming and acid rain.

Reuse packaging

Try and buy products with minimal packaging. A simple step is to reuse plastic bags at supermarkets. Also read the labelling of products carefully as the term 'environmentally friendly' has become confused and abused. Try and avoid using large amounts of detergent and bleach.

Buy more organically produced foodstuffs

More and more of our foods are being genetically interfered with and new strains produced. Organically produced foods avoid this problem as well as the damage caused by agrochemicals but have the disadvantage of being more expensive. However, we should remember that this is because they are often produced by labour-intensive means which is providing fairly paid work for many. If buying meat we can choose to buy either from farm shops or use particular butchers where we can be sure that the animals were genuinely 'free range'.

Keep God as your main priority

When considering these points all of us will respond differently. It is no good spending hours trying to find nothing but ethically produced products if it totally destroys our budget, means we stop giving or stop enjoying the life God has given us. It is important that the pursuit of such goals doesn't become such an obsession that it replaces God as your main priority in either time or energy.

Being a committed Christian involves making lots of difficult choices. It also means we must strive and get the balance right.

We need to tell people about Jesus but at the same time use our resources wisely so that we are being good stewards financially without exploiting anyone in so doing. To do this requires courage, commitment and acceptance that this will turn our lives around completely. We are called to store up treasures in Heaven so why do so many of us try to store up treasures on earth?

The National Lottery

> Donations to charities fell by £71 million in the first four months after the introduction of the Lottery.

Having written so much about the needs of the Third World earlier in this chapter I find it hard to write about the National Lottery. By encouraging it the Government has also encouraged a 'get-something-for-nearly-nothing' and a 'get-rich-quick' philosophy to accelerate in our nation. Since its introduction giving to charities has declined steeply – to such an extent that invaluable workers have been made redundant and cutbacks in essential work have taken place.

I don't want to appear to be a killjoy, but buying a few lottery tickets or scratch cards is not just having a bit of fun. First, it is appalling stewardship. The chances of winning are extremely remote and for every ticket you purchase only 5.6p goes to charity so there can really be no justification that charitable giving is a motive for buying lottery tickets. Second, it increases gambling and addiction. It is easy to see why. Once you have picked your six numbers you are petrified that if you miss just one week that will be the time when they come up. Of course, this is total nonsense, but it is the sort of irrational fear that gambling is built on. Gamblers Anonymous have reported a sharp rise in calls to their helpline since the Lottery came into being – with sadly a considerable number of teenagers addicted to scratch cards. Experts on gambling say that scratch cards are deliberately designed to keep people playing by offering small prizes, or figures that *nearly* get the jackpot. This persuades people they are 'lucky'. As many people scratch their cards while still in the vicinity of the shop they are thus induced to buy more cards. They often end up losing more than if they had stopped initially. Camelot denies the cards are compulsive, saying they are usually an 'impulse buy'.

It is also true that it encourages those who are really struggling with money to buy tickets. In desperation they think that if only they won on the lottery all their troubles would be over. So they buy tickets they cannot afford, don't win and eventually end up even deeper in debt. We have had several calls on our helpline from distraught people whose partners have used up all their spending allowance on tickets so there is nothing left to feed the family for the rest of the week.

There have also been tragic cases. One man on checking his regular numbers believed he had won about £2 million and then he suddenly realized that this particular week he had forgotten to buy the ticket. In desperation he shot himself. A moment of madness had deprived a family of a husband and father. The amount he actually would have won was . . . £27.

Not so tragic but showing how ridiculously easy it is to get hooked is the following story. A family were due to fly abroad on holiday. Arriving at the airport early the father disappeared to buy some magazines for the flight. Two hours later he reappeared with a sorry tale to tell. He had bought some scratch cards and won £10 so he decided to buy some more. Eventually he cleared the shop of all their scratch cards, spending about £500 in the process. He had blown their holiday spending money on nothing.

Sadly, many Christians are buying lottery tickets with no regard for the harm it can do to others. Even if we feel we can afford the occasional 'flutter' we should not be wasting God's money in this way. Also by doing so we can so easily 'cause our weaker brother to stumble' (cf. Romans 14.13), and we are explicitly called to avoid doing anything that would cause this to happen. I believe many Christians who buy tickets do feel guilty about doing so. Only recently a lady phoned our helpline. She was 78 years old and on a widow's pension. She said that on many weeks after paying for food, rent, etc. she had nothing left to give to the church but occasionally if she had a little left over she would buy a lottery ticket because, if she won, she would be able to give a large amount to the church. I talked to her about the story of the widow's mite and said that on the week that she could afford it, it would be better to simply give the £1 to the church because she was in fact giving all she had. The dear lady burst into tears of relief. 'I have felt so bad buying these things,' she said, 'but I could see no other alternative.' How we need sound financial teaching in our churches!

Unfortunately we are unlikely to get it when we see some churches actually applying to the lottery for funding. A spokesman for one actually said, 'I'm afraid we have no option.' Isn't prayer an option? How about fasting? What about teaching their members the joys of hilarious giving?

So as we conclude this chapter it is important to remember that we need to be aware of the ethical, ecological and environmental impact that our spending can have on others. As with Traidcraft, it can be very positive or, with the Lottery, it can be destructive. The Bible is very clear which way we must go. Look again at Luke 16.10–11 (see p. 29).

Ask yourself

1 Do I handle money ethically?
2 Am I aware of what long-term environmental impact my spending is having?
3 Have I considered how my money is used? Could it be invested in more ethical ways?
4 Do I do all I can to ensure that none of my purchases exploit anybody anywhere in the world?

9 FINAL PERSPECTIVES

We have already noted the surprising fact that there is more recorded in the Bible about the way we handle our money and possessions than about any other aspect of Christian living. Like everything else money and possessions can have a positive or a negative usage. As Christians we need to be using them to help glorify God. I believe no aspect of life is more important in determining whether we are living in the perfect will of God.

The reason for this is clear. For us in our materialistic society no sin can seduce us as subtly and speedily as materialism. If you are committing adultery then it is clear that you are sinning and you need to deal with that sin with genuine repentance and altered behaviour. But where are the similar responses when it comes to selfish, materialistic behaviour? No sin is explained away more rationally. But we need to trust God more and put Him first in the area of finances as in all others. If we simply do this God will honour our obedience, raise our faith levels and meet us at the point of our need.

Wealth

Money can be so seductive. It is easy to say we trust God, when our actions indicate that our trust is in our own wealth. Riches can so easily erode our faith. We can possess many things and use them for the glory of God but we are so easily tempted to love what we have. There are several dangers to having significant wealth:

Wealth tends to separate people from each other

'Abram had become very wealthy in livestock and silver and gold. Now Lot . . . also had flocks and herds and tents. But the land could not support them both while they stayed together, for their possessions were so great they were not able to stay together. And quarrelling arose between Abram's herdsmen and the herdsmen of Lot' (Genesis 13.2, 5–7 NIV).

Wealth caused separation between Abram and Lot and it can still have the same impact when relationships deteriorate as family members fight over money and possessions.

Wealth can easily make us arrogant

'Command those who are rich in this present world not to be arrogant nor to put their hope in wealth, which is so uncertain, but to put their hope in God who richly provides us with everything for our enjoyment' (1 Timothy 6.17 NIV).

Wealth can make us forget God

You only have to read the Bible thoroughly to see that many times when God has blessed His people, they have become wealthy. Rather than thanking God for pouring out the blessings on them, they have become self-sufficient, taken God for granted and assumed they had no further need of Him.

'When I have brought them into the land flowing with milk and honey, the land I promised on oath to their forefathers, and when they eat their fill and thrive, they will turn to other gods and worship them, rejecting me and breaking my covenant.' (Deuteronomy 31.20 NIV)

Wealth makes it harder to come to know Jesus as Saviour

'Jesus said to his disciples, "I tell you the truth, it is hard for a rich man to enter the kingdom of heaven"' (Matthew 19.23 NIV).

Riches deceive because they are obvious and visible and can thus so easily blind us to the unseen realities of God. On the surface they appear to be able to do what in fact only Jesus can do – provide for all our needs, bring contentment and give us peace of mind.

In the parable of the sower Jesus said: 'The one who received the seed that fell among the thorns is the man who hears the word, but the worries of this life and the deceitfulness of wealth choke it, making it unfruitful' (Matthew 13.22 NIV).

Coveting and greed

Coveting and greed have been with us since the beginning of time. Coveting means to desire or be jealous of another person's prosperity. Greed means constantly to want more. In the story of creation there was only one thing that Eve could not have and yet she felt she just had to have it. The last of the ten commandments expressly forbids us to be greedy. 'You shall not covet your neighbour's house. You shall not covet your neighbour's wife, or his manservant or maidservant, his ox or donkey, or anything that belongs to your neighbour' (Exodus 20.17 NIV). In other words we are told we should not covet *anything* that belongs to anyone else.

A greedy or covetous person is an idolater and according to Ephesians 5.5 has 'no inheritance in the kingdom of Christ and God'. Jesus was constantly warning His followers not to stumble and succumb to the temptations of money. Indeed when He saw financial abuse and greed actually taking place in the name of religion He got extremely angry and overturned the money-changers' tables in the temple. Shortly before he died, Paul wrote to Timothy: 'There will be terrible times in the last days. People will be lovers of themselves, lovers of money, . . . lovers of pleasure rather than lovers of God – having a form of godliness but denying its power. Have nothing to do with them' (2 Timothy 3.1–2, 4–5 NIV). Doesn't this sound like society today? Sadly, these characteristics are increasingly spilling over into our churches. We need to face up to this and as Christians fight it head on.

Jesus made it very clear that it is possible to be lulled into complacency and worldly ways by society's affluence. This is why the Laodicean church was criticized so strongly (see Revelation 3.17, quoted on p. 164). We are so like this today –

never having had so much materially and in relative terms never having given so little. Like the church in Laodicea we need refined gold (which signifies faith), white clothes to wear (indicating purity and holiness) and 'eyes that can see' how materialistic and greedy we have become. The good news is that Jesus says there is still time for us to repent. We *can* be restored and renewed.

As long as we remember that coveting and greed are likely to be prevalent in the West we can start to detest them for what they really are. We are called to surrender everything to follow Jesus. It is our attitude of heart that matters, not whether we are actually rich or poor. I have known people who are poor and greedy, and others who are rich, yet totally free from greed or the desire to cling on to wealth. It is not a sin to possess riches but they can be so seductive, and whatever somebody else has can be so attractive. So it is the love of money and possessions that can become gods and replace Jesus as our Lord of *all*. It is important therefore that we start discarding all this excess baggage. So often an attempt to control our material situation reflects a lack of spiritual security. Unless we totally believe in the sufficiency of God and His love for us we will lose our purpose and become just like the rest of this 'me-centred' world. We do not become 'somebody' by having. We become 'somebody' by giving.

Contentment

All that we long for is to be found in Christ alone. 1 Timothy 6.8 has always really challenged me: 'And if we have food and clothing we will be content with that' (NASB). What God is saying here is that we should be content if our basic needs are being met. Our society says something different. If you can afford to wear the latest fashions, drive a new luxury car, holiday in exotic locations and live in a beautiful home in the best neighbourhood you will be happy – but you'll probably want a yacht! The whole fabric of our society is based on materialism and consumerism. It operates on two assumptions – that more is always better and that happiness is based on the acquisition of things. I believe this is totally wrong. Rich and poor alike long for real love and intimacy and it is only our Lord who can provide this.

The word 'contentment' appears seven times in the Bible and on six occasions it is in relation to money. Look at Philippians 4.11–13. Twice in this passage Paul says he has had to *learn* to be content. It is not something we are born with. As far as I can ascertain there are three elements to contentment:

- Know what God requires of you.
- Fulfil those requirements.
- Trust God to do His part.

Contentment does *not* mean just sitting back and doing nothing. There is nothing wrong with God-given motivated ambition. God wants us to work hard as we aim to be ever-increasingly faithful stewards of the talents and possessions that He has given to us. Biblical contentment is that inner peace that accepts whatever God provides for us, knowing that He has perfect plans for each one. Hebrews 13.5 tells us why: 'Keep your lives free from the love of money and be content with what you have, because God has said, "Never will I leave you, never will I forsake you"' (NIV).

Money or the abundance of material things does not make someone what God meant him or her to be. All possessions are meaningless when compared to spiritual riches. What we truly own is that which death cannot take away, which others cannot steal and which 'moth and rust' cannot taint. Money can never hold you, comfort you, tell you 'I love you' – even though we often try and buy or show love with it. We need to be truly content.

> Let me hold lightly to the things of this earth,
> Transient treasures, what are they worth?
> Moths can corrupt them; rust can decay,
> All their bright beauty fades in a day.
> Let me hold lightly temporal things –
> I, who am deathless, I who wear wings!
> Let me hold fast, Lord, things of the skies,
> Quicken my vision, open my eyes!

> Show me thy riches, glory and grace,
> Boundless as time is, endless as space,
> Let me hold lightly things that were mine –
> Lord, thou dost give me all that is thine.
>
> Martha Snell Nicholson

Lifestyle

The test of true repentance is a permanent change in the pattern of our behaviour. The purpose of the Body of Christ is to make Jesus visible to a world who cannot see Him. This means not only telling people about Him but living out Jesus' love, mercy and hope in a needy and lost world. It has been said that no one can hate someone who truly loves, and this is certainly true of any Christian who is unselfish and generous with their material possessions. We are, therefore, to be witnesses to others through the way we use our material resources, demonstrating that it is Jesus, not money, who rules all parts of our lives. Our world needs to be amazed by love rather than sunk with evil. To reverse worldly values is costly to a Christian, but if we do not act out the teaching we have received from Jesus we are being disobedient. However, what makes it particularly hard is that there is no standard lifestyle laid down in the Bible. It is not that easy! God puts His people in all societies and at every level. This means that each one of us needs to evaluate our standard of living prayerfully. To help us do this I have listed some biblical principles to follow.

Constantly concentrate on an eternal perspective

Our society thrusts a 'now' mentality down our throat. Advertisers persuade prospective purchasers to buy things straight away, giving no thought to any potential problems tomorrow. It is important to remember that our time on earth is but a blink of an eye when compared with eternity. Yet how we handle our money today can make a big difference in eternity. We not only have the privilege of storing up treasures for ourselves in heaven but we also are able to use our money to help win the lost. Gaining an eternal perspective and eternal values will have a radical effect on decision-making. Moses is a good example of this. Look at Hebrews 11.24–6. Moses had a choice between earthly rewards and an eternal reward. As the adopted son of Pharaoh's daughter he could either enjoy a lavish lifestyle or he could choose to become a Hebrew slave. Because he had an eternal perspective he chose the latter and was thus able to be used by God in a remarkable way. Many things that seem important to us now will fade into total insignificance when we get to heaven. We have to choose between looking heavenward and focusing on the here and now.

Never say 'if only'

It is so easy to think 'if only'. 'If only I had more money or a better job then I could really do things for God.' 'If only I could win the lottery!' Being used by God has nothing to do with having money or position. It has everything to do with a willingness to allow Jesus to become Lord of our lives.

Do not determine your lifestyle in comparison to others

One of the main reasons for not putting God first and overspending is because people are trying to 'keep up with the Joneses'. This is always an impossible task because you can never quite catch up with their spending habits. If you are relatively wealthy you do not have to live at your maximum level of expenditure. Listen to when God tells you 'enough is enough'.

Prayerfully submit all spending decisions to God

As everything we possess is owned by God, we should spend to please Him rather than for selfish purposes. This does *not* mean that He will only ever allow us to buy the bare necessities.

Do not allow your lifestyle to cause others to stumble

'Make up your own mind not to put any stumbling block or obstacle in your brother's way' (Romans 14.13 NIV). Always be aware of the impact that the way you spend your money will have on others. Of course, this is particularly true of people in leadership positions.

Ask yourself how much is enough

Once you have achieved all your God-given financial goals, consider giving away everything you earn above them. Alternatively, you could work voluntarily for an organization which otherwise could not afford to employ you.

Make every effort to live more simply

Possessions usually require time, attention and money to maintain them. Too many of the wrong types of things can demand so much from us that they can easily harm our relationships with both God and family. An uncomplicated lifestyle spares us time for each other and for God. 'Make it your ambition to lead a quiet life, to mind your own business and to work with your hands, just as we told you, so that your daily life may win the respect of outsiders and so that you will not be dependent on anybody' (1 Thessalonians 4.11–12 NIV).

Although lifestyles of individuals can be very different, everyone should have their basic needs met.

> Our desire is not that others might be relieved while you are hard pressed, but that there might be equality. At the present time your plenty will supply what they need, so that in turn their plenty will supply what you need. Then there will be equality, as it is written, 'He who gathered much did not have too much and he who gathered little did not have too little'. (2 Corinthians 8.13–15 NIV).

Look too at how the early disciples lived.

> All the believers were together and had everything in common. Selling their possessions and goods, they gave to anyone as he had need. (Acts 2.44–5 NIV)

> All the believers were one in heart and mind. No-one claimed that any of his possessions was his own, but they shared everything they had. With great power the apostles continued to testify to the resurrection of the Lord Jesus, and much grace was upon them all. There were no needy persons among them. For from time to time those who owned land or houses sold them, brought the money from the sales and put it at the apostles' feet, and it was distributed to anyone as he had need. (Acts 4.32–5 NIV)

Money is meaningless compared to knowing Jesus

The pursuit of wealth can destroy an intimate relationship with Jesus. 'What good is it for a man to gain the whole world, yet forfeit his soul?' (Mark 8.36 NIV).

We are in a spiritual battle

'For our struggle is not against flesh and blood but against . . . the spiritual forces of evil in the heavenly realms' (Ephesians 6.12 NIV). In any battle you use your most effective weapons. The devil's prime aim is to stop us serving Jesus effectively and in our society he therefore tempts us to serve money and possessions instead. For most of us money will be the major competitor with Christ for the lordship of our lives. 'You cannot serve both God and Money' (Matthew 6.24 NIV). In our society it is respectable to love money – the government even encourages us to gamble to get more of it. People may congratulate you and envy the trappings of your financial success. Please pray about your relationship with money.

Do not conform to the world

Romans 12.2 tells us: 'Do not conform any longer to the pattern of this world' (NIV). We live in one of the most affluent societies the world has ever known. We are constantly bombarded with manipulative advertising. We are told that we can have a beautifully fulfilled life, but we have to buy it. It has been said that many people buy things they don't need with money they don't have to impress people they don't like!

If our lives do not look significantly different to our counterparts', that is, if we have not lived as simply as we can, shared more keenly and loved more openly, then perhaps we have not really let the words of Jesus sink into our hearts. On Judgement Day we will not be asked where we lived or about our car but about how we responded to the hungry, homeless and hurting.

Most of us are spending more than we earn. This creates pressure, anxiety and significant financial bondage. Inability to reach the paradise promised by the advertisers only increases the envy and discontent. We must be careful! From time to time we are likely to get hooked on something we are sure we must buy. Once hooked it is so easy to rationalize the purchase away. So when faced with a major spending decision, remember to seek God's guidance and use the advice of a spiritually mature person as confirmation.

Poverty, prosperity or stewardship

Some Christians live at extreme levels of finances. There will be those who argue that if you are truly spiritual you must be poor, because it is impossible to have a close relationship with Jesus if you are wealthy. Believers of the opposite view consider that if a Christian is genuinely walking in faith he or she will enjoy uninterrupted prosperity.

Poverty

God does not expect His people to live in poverty. Money and possessions are morally neutral and can be used for either good or evil. A number of godly people in the Bible were among the wealthiest of their day. What is more, there are clear examples in the Old Testament of God rewarding His children when they obeyed Him. Psalm 35.27 says, 'The Lord ... delights in the well-being of his servant' (NIV). As our faith grows and our giving becomes sacrificial so God may well choose to bless us. A godly person can have material resources.

Prosperity

There are some who believe that all who truly believe will really prosper. This too is wrong. The guidelines for any prosperity we may have are found in Joshua 1.8: 'Do not let this Book of the Law depart from your mouth; meditate on it day and night, so that you may be careful to do everything written in it. *Then* you will be prosperous and successful' (NIV). There are therefore two requirements for prosperity – you must consistently meditate on and learn the Bible, and also act out carefully what is written in it. Once you have fulfilled these two obligations you have put yourself in a position where you could be blessed financially. However, there is absolutely no guarantee that even in this position we will experience such prosperity. Some reasons for this are:

A violation of a biblical principle
Look again at Joshua 1.8 – we must do it *all.*

Character-building
Romans 5.3–4 says, 'Suffering brings perseverance, and perseverance character' (NASB). Many very godly people went through times when they lost all their possessions even though they were living as they should. David had to flee for his life from King Saul leaving everything behind. Job lost his family and possessions in an instant but was still described as 'blameless and upright, a man who fears God and shuns evil' (Job 1.8 NIV). Paul was a prisoner and knew want. God sometimes lets difficult circumstances enter our lives so that He can build our character. If I give

my children too much they will be spoilt and their characters badly damaged. Finding maturity is a slow and often painful process. The best example of this is found in Deuteronomy 8.16–18.

> 'He gave you manna to eat in the desert, something your fore-fathers had never known, to humble and to test you so that in the end it might go well with you. You may say to yourself, "My power and the strength of my hands have produced this wealth for me." But remember the Lord your God, for it is he who gives you the ability to produce wealth, and so confirms his covenant, which he swore to your forefathers, as it is today.' (NIV)

The Children of Israel had to be humbled before the Lord knew they were ready to handle wealth.

Our loving Father knows us better than we know ourselves and He knows exactly how much He can entrust to us at any one time without it harming our relationship with Him.

God's discipline
'He punishes everyone he accepts as a son . . . for our good that we may share in his holiness' (Hebrews 12.6, 10 NIV).

To help us recognize our dependence
When our possessions are few or even non-existent it becomes easier to recognize our need of our Heavenly Father. At these times we have Him alone to hold on to. I know of many Christians who have turned to God in times of financial crisis – some even making the commitment to Jesus because of it.

Because He is sovereign
We want to recognize that God is fully sovereign, and ultimately He will choose how much to entrust to each person at any one time.

It is important to see that God's evaluation of true riches differs much from the world's view. This is clearly shown in

Revelation. Compare these two verses: 'I know your afflictions and your poverty – yet you are rich!' (Revelation 2.9 NIV). 'You say, "I am rich, I have acquired wealth and do not need a thing." But you do not realize that you are wretched, pitiful, poor, blind and naked' (Revelation 3.17 NIV). The godly poor are rich in God's sight but those who are wealthy and do not have a close relationship with Jesus are actually poor. True prosperity goes way beyond material possessions. It is gauged by how well we know Jesus and how clearly we are following Him.

So we need to be on our guard against those who are trying to deceive us as they promote the 'prosperity gospel'. Not only do they appeal to our God-given desire to be obedient to Him by giving but they also appeal to our natural human desires to be blessed materially. Consequently prosperity teaching promotes a gospel of putting self first and has at the same time, through using questionable fund-raising methods, lined the pockets of several of its leading proponents. Nowhere in the Bible are we told to give so that we can gain earthly treasures in return. Giving is to be motivated by an unselfish heart that is willing to share unconditionally with those in need, regardless of monetary return. God will reward us in heaven to the degree of sacrifice we have made.

There is therefore no need to worry if the wicked appear to prosper. Psalm 37.1–2 says: 'Do not fret because of evil men or be envious of those who do wrong; for like the grass they will soon wither, like green plants they will soon die away' (NIV). It is far more important to keep God's eternal perspective in the forefront of our minds.

Stewardship

'Everything which hinders us from loving God above all things and acts as a barrier between ourselves and our obedience to Jesus is our treasure and the place where our heart is.' (Dietrich Bonhoeffer, 1906–1945, German theologian)

We will only know best how to manage our money when we put God firmly on the throne as Master of all. We must put God at the forefront of all our planning and then determine to live our lives on earth understanding that all we are and all we have comes from Him. We have no justification in taking credit for any accomplishments – the more God blesses us the more we should praise and thank Him. If our achievements do include the acquisition of wealth, we should not concentrate on building a temporary kingdom for ourselves but rather we should give generously because we want to see the Kingdom of God extended.

I believe that those who have demonstrated generosity will inherit this Kingdom. Repeatedly Jesus shows two opposing ways of looking at things here on earth – either from an earthly or heavenly perspective. We cannot look both ways at the same time. Jesus' definition of treasure is that which enthrals us the most and towards which we devote by far and away our greatest efforts. He is, in effect, asking what matters most to us, how this affects us and where our eyes are really focused. As long as we are struggling to decide between heavenly and earthly things our judgement will be questionable as we are unable to 'see' things as God sees them.

> 'It is want of faith that makes us opt for earthly rather than heavenly treasure. If we really believed in celestial treasures who among us would be so stupid as to buy gold? We just do not believe. Heaven is a dream, a religious fantasy which we affirm because we are orthodox. If people believed in heaven they would spend their time preparing for permanent residence there. But nobody does. We just like the assurance that something nice awaits us when the real life is over.' (*Money Isn't God, So Why Are We Worshipping It?*, John White, Canadian psychiatrist and Christian writer)

Sadly, we have largely failed in our roles as stewards. We have overvalued material prosperity and have underestimated, taken for granted or even totally forgotten the God of love and power we claim to worship. We say we have faith in Him but as long as we feel anxious about our financial situation or are impressed by the importance of money, our voices have a hollow ring about them. Real faith in the invisible God can only be demonstrated by having complete control over material things and thus preventing them from controlling us in any way.

As we aim to achieve the proper balance between poverty and prosperity we need to recall that it is only the person of Jesus who can both inspire and challenge us to reach out for love, holiness, truth and contentment. This is true Christian stewardship. Table 15 helps put this into perspective.

Table 15

	Poverty	Stewardship	Prosperity
Possessions are:	evil	a responsibility	a right
I work to:	cover basic needs	serve Christ	get rich
Godly people are:	poor	faithful	rich
Ungodly people are:	rich	faithless	poor
I give:	because I must	because I love God	to get
My spending is:	without gratitude	prayerful and responsible	carefree and careless

Taxes

Jesus was specifically asked about paying taxes so this is easy to answer.

> 'Is it right for us to pay taxes to Caesar or not?' He saw through their duplicity and said to them 'Show me a denarius. Whose portrait and inscription are on it?' 'Caesar's,' they replied. He said to them, 'Then give to Caesar what is Caesar's, and to God what is God's.' (Luke 20.22–5 NIV)

Whatever we may think about the way the government spends our taxes we must still 'submit to the authorities . . . for the authorities are God's servants who give their full time to governing.

Give everyone what you owe him; if you owe taxes, pay taxes' (Romans 13.5–7 NIV). However, we must know where our money goes and be prepared to speak out if we object to the way it is being used. To object to taxation being used in wrong ways the best thing to do is write to your MP at the House of Commons, Westminster, London, SW1A 0AA. (It is estimated that an MP will consider your view to represent 1,000 people as so few bother to write!) You should also use schemes such as Gift Aid and covenants to the best possible effect. The government is actually encouraging you to maximize and prioritize your giving.

Partiality

This is an area where it is so easy for wealth to invade. Anyone who is able to help the helpless but refuses to do so shows partiality and is also being unjust. In the Body of Christ every member is important. Just because some people do not have a significant number of possessions does not mean they are of any less value. We must therefore never put the poor in a lower position because of their economic conditions. This shows discrimination and has nothing to do with our Christian faith.

Whenever we show deference to those who are wealthy, or for that matter have any kind of prominence, be it financial, academic or even spiritual, we are guilty of showing favour. The first few verses of James chapter 2 show this clearly. The best way to overcome partiality is to concentrate on the positive strengths and abilities of each person. Everybody can do some things a lot better than I can and every person has talents and attributes that I lack. I can thus appreciate everybody.

Conclusion

Money is one of the most talked about subjects in the Bible and there are three main spiritual reasons for this:

- How we handle our money affects our relationship with Jesus.

- Money is the main competitor with Jesus for the lordship of our life.
- The way we handle our money moulds our character.

Simply knowing the biblical principles for handling money is not enough. We have to act on this knowledge. Jesus said:

'Everyone who hears these words of mine and puts them into practice is like a wise man who built his house on the rock. The rain came down, the streams rose, and the winds blew and beat against that house; yet it did not fall, because it had its foundation on the rock. But everyone who hears these words of mine and does not put them into practice is like a foolish man who built his house on sand. The rain came down, the streams rose, and the winds blew and beat against that house, and it fell with a great crash.' (Matthew 7.24–7 NIV)

If we have built our house on the solid principles found in the Bible it will not fall. One of the best ways to demonstrate your love for your family is to get your financial house in order.

So how do we recognize people who have their financial house in order and are handling money God's way? These are the people who are giving regularly, systematically and proportionately. They are not defensive about money – in fact they are as excited about the biblical teaching in this area as in all other areas. They enjoy the things that God has given to them for their enjoyment and benefit, but they never love these things more than they love God. They are not materialistic, and neither are they proud or arrogant. They are seeking first the Kingdom of God, loving people, not things.

Our aim too should be to be like Jesus, to spread His good news, to share His love in a desperately needy world, and to show His power. It is 'our' finances that will help ensure this happens. Money is needed to take the gospel to all parts of the world, to help set people free and bring eternal peace to them. Finance will provide books, Bible translations and the support of teaching, pastoral and evangelistic ministries.

We will be in heaven before the final result of everything we ever did and gave will be revealed to us. Every penny I gave, every word I ever said as a witness, every prayer I have ever prayed, everything I have ever written or said over the phone, every visit I have made – all will be there to show me who I influenced for Christ. However small it is, what we are doing for Jesus on earth will have its heavenly reward – and it will stay with us for ever.

I pray that you will be able to use this book so that you can become financially faithful in day-to-day practical matters. This will undoubtedly take time. Whatever you do, do not give up the goal of being debt-free or giving or saving more because it looks impossible. It is your responsibility to make a genuine effort to improve – no matter how small that improvement may appear – and then let God pour out His love and support as He leads you on. Do not get discouraged. Be faithful. We serve a wonderful God.

Ask yourself

1 Am I using my material possessions as God intended?
2 What do I think about most?
3 What takes up most of my emotional and physical energy?
4 How do I respond when I see human needs?
5 How do I feel when I am 'nudged' to give away money or possessions that are more needed by someone else?
6 How do the following influence my lifestyle and spending patterns: – comparing my lifestyle with that of my friends and others? – television? – newspapers, magazines and advertisements? – the Bible? – my commitment to Christ's priorities?
7 Do I think God would have me alter my lifestyle in any way? If so, how?
8 Do I understand the fallacy of prosperity teaching, but yet at the same time understand the real blessing that God wants to give out to those who are faithful in their giving?
9 Do I show genuine humility with poorer Christians?
10 What would I do if I inherited £25,000 today?

USEFUL ADDRESSES

Care for the Family	136 Newport Road, Cardiff CF2 1DJ
Christian Service Centre	Holloway Street West, Lower Gornal, Dudley, W. Midlands DY3 2DZ
Credit Action	6 Regent Terrace, Cambridge CB2 1AA
Ethical Financial	316 House, 7 Tyverlon Business Park, Barry, S. Glamorgan CF6 3BE
Jubilee Centre	3 Hooper Street, Cambridge CB1 2NZ
Sovereign Giving	6 Heatherwood Close, Thorpe End, Norwich NR1 5BN
Tear Fund	100 Church Road, Teddington, Middlesex TW11 8QE
Traidcraft plc	Kingsway, Gateshead, Tyne and Wear
United Kingdom Evangelization Trust (UKET)	PO Box 99, Loughton, Essex 1G10 3QJ